In the Fullness of Time

In the Fullness of Time

A story from the past and future of the church

Paul Bradbury

CANTERBURY PRESS

Norwich

© Paul Bradbury 2024

Published in 2024 by Canterbury Press
Editorial office
3rd Floor, Invicta House,
110 Golden Lane,
London EC1Y 0TG, UK
www.canterburypress.co.uk

Canterbury Press is an imprint of Hymns Ancient & Modern Ltd
(a registered charity)

Hymns Ancient & Modern

Hymns Ancient & Modern® is a registered trademark of
Hymns Ancient & Modern Ltd
13A Hellesdon Park Road, Norwich,
Norfolk NR6 5DR, UK

All rights reserved. No part of this publication may be reproduced,
stored in a retrieval system, or transmitted,
in any form or by any means, electronic, mechanical,
photocopying or otherwise, without the prior permission of
the publisher, SCM Press.

The Author has asserted his right under the Copyright, Designs and
Patents Act 1988 to be identified as the Author of this Work

Scripture quotations taken from the Holy Bible, New International
Version. Copyright © 1973, 1978, 1984, 2011 by Biblica, Inc.
Used by permission of Zondervan. All rights reserved worldwide.

British Library Cataloguing in Publication data

A catalogue record for this book is available
from the British Library

ISBN 978 1 78622 607 5

Typeset by Regent Typesetting
Printed and bound by
CPI Group (UK) Ltd

*For my mother,
with thanks*

Contents

Acknowledgements — xi
Introduction — xiii

Part 1 Lamentation

The Lighthouse – A Parable — 3
1 All Saints, Stour Row, Dorset — 5
2 St Catherine's Chapel, Milton Abbas, Dorset — 17
3 St Mary's, Drimpton, Beaminster Team Ministry — 30

Part 2 Waiting

The Manual and the Measure – A Parable — 45
4 Oak Tree Anglican Fellowship, Acton, London — 47
5 St Alban's, Norwich — 61

Part 3 Resurrection

The Farm – A Parable — 77
6 Bardney Missional Community, Lincolnshire — 79
7 Garden Church, Great Melton, Norfolk — 95
8 East Holme Priory, Dorset — 111

Further Resources — 135
Bibliography — 137

'Above all, trust in the slow work of God.'

Pierre Teilhard de Chardin SJ

Acknowledgements

The genesis of this book came from an illness and a gift. Two years ago I was ill over New Year and took to the sofa with James Rebanks' *English Pastoral*. I forget who gave it to me – if it was you, thank you. The book inspired me to think it might be possible to tell a story about the church in a similar way to how Rebanks tells a story about farming. A story in which the common concerns of tradition, love, survival and place rise above entrenched positions and divisions around methods.

Huge thanks must go to those who were willing to tell their stories as part of the research for this book: Richard and Barbara Priest, Lewis Pearson, Jo Neary, David Baldwin, David Lloyd, Pete Atkins, Charlotte Bayes, Hilary Bond, Lucy Bolster, Ben Lucas and John Good. I hope my retelling and reflections do justice to their stories and insights offered with honesty and generosity.

The development of the book benefitted immensely from the time, attention and insights of those willing to read a draft version – Steve Aisthorpe, Andrew Rumsey, Jonny Baker, Tim Thorlby, Howard Peskett, Anne Long, Karen Gorham and Stephen Lake. Thanks in particular to Andrew Rumsey for his enthusiastic advocacy for the book.

Hilary and Will Bond generously allowed me to spend time at East Holme Priory. Will provided me with detailed information on the history of the Priory and the archaeological research that has been conducted there – thank you.

I am grateful to Jenny Wills and all at Christ the King Anglican Church in the Algarve for their welcome and support while I was a locum minister for two weeks and able to give much time to writing. Thanks in particular to Richard and Jo Lee for the use of their beautiful house in Loulé, which was a cool, quiet and fruitful place to allow this book to take shape.

Thanks to the hugely talented Harry Taylor for the beautiful sketches that accompany each chapter (follow him on Instagram: @hzza_art, he has a bright future!).

I'm grateful to David Shervington, Mary Matthews and the team at Canterbury Press for their gracious and skilled navigation through the process from the initial manuscript to what you hold in your hands.

And, as ever, huge thanks to my wife Emily for always encouraging me, believing that I have something to say that's worth saying.

Introduction

I'm in a borrowed car. A large and powerful borrowed car that makes me feel conspicuous and uncomfortable. The sense of discomfort grows as I leave the main road and head into the little lanes that I know so well. This is home territory. I am retracing a route that I must have done hundreds of times between my home in the Blackmoor Vale, Dorset, and my school some seven miles away. I know every little kink and deviation, every rise and fall, every farm and barn, stream and copse. Certain points on the route bring memories back immediately – usually places where we narrowly missed a collision with a tractor or some other slow-moving obstacle, like a cow. My route to school was monotonous, but it was rarely dull.

I drop down the sharp hill about a mile from the village and pick up the lane that heads up the long gentle slope to where I grew up. The final stretch toward the village was always the most narrow and dangerous. I creep round each bend conscious that, despite the fallback of insurance, it wouldn't do to prang this impressive machine on my first outing with it. With relief I head out of that section and further up the lane, where the cottages of the village begin. I feel awkward, like the village kid made good returning in a flash car to flaunt the hard-won riches of the wider world over his humble rural origins. I drive into the main street, park there and begin walking back towards the church and the lane where we used to live. I feel that odd mix of stranger and local. Nothing has changed and yet everything feels a little unfamiliar, as though the place has been occupied by a different tribe of people who have now settled and made the place theirs.

It is 14 years since I was in Stour Row. On that occasion we buried my father's ashes in the graveyard of the small parish church at the top our lane. It was my father who brought our family to this village in the early 1980s. He was a builder who had run a good business in Bournemouth. When his business partner sadly died my father decided to sell up. After a brief dalliance with the hotel trade, our family then moved from Bournemouth out to the country, buying this large country house with acres of garden. It was bliss. Masses of space to explore, trees to climb, a vast lawn to play cricket with kids from neighbouring houses. And then a few years later we moved again. The cost and time needed to maintain a house like that proved too much. And so we came to the village that would be the place that shaped my most formative years. This was home through the end of primary school and into the whole of secondary school until I went away to university and, to all intents and purposes, left for good.

My experience of living here was somehow always coloured by nostalgia for where we had moved from. Stour Row is small, very small. There were few other families. The house was smaller and it had a relatively small garden. Instead of cycling with other families to my local primary school, I walked to the end of the farm track where a bus picked up me and another child from the village and ferried us the three or so miles there and back. Not long after that, however, I was awarded a scholarship to a local private school. And so began the years of journeying through the lanes of north Dorset to school and back each day. It was this development that started a gradual drift away from the village that was my home. School, with its long days, Saturday morning lessons and afternoon sports, Sunday afternoon choir rehearsal and chapel service, more and more provided a kind of alternative world. The village, by comparison, had little to offer me – few other children, no meaningful public transport, nothing to do except ramble about the fields and woods, and there was only so long you could do that for.

And yet Stour Row did something within me in those years, years when in every other respect I was starting to look elsewhere. As I now walked along the familiar main street of the

INTRODUCTION

village, I realized how that something had gone very deep indeed. This village, with its dull and unremarkable rows of cottages infilled with uninspiring bungalows and cul-de-sacs of new development, had become in those years a place that knew me, a place that somehow held me and nurtured me in those tricky years of adolescence. Like so many small villages, Stour Row was that place where you were known. A place where adults followed your progress and somehow championed your small wins and growing potential in the world. A place that held you in its delicate web of relationships and acquaintances, common knowledge and shared experience. And I realize that in many ways, for the rest of my life, I've been looking for and trying to create something that feels much like that.

I turn from the main street and into the lane where the line of dwellings that includes our house stretches down the gently sloping lane away from the village. It quickly becomes clear that much has changed. The row of old cottages, with their long narrow gardens, remains. But it feels like the generation of mostly ex-farm labourers who occupied them when I was growing up has gone. Most of the cottages have been enlarged. Many have taken advantage of the offer of extending their land outward into the fields. And each house is now replete with that particular symbol of growth and affluence: security technology. Alarms, cameras and warning signs are fixed on the outside of these cottages, now seemingly turned inwards from the threat of the outside world and toward the private fiefdom within.

But perhaps I'm getting cynical in my own nostalgia. And what has brought me here except nostalgia? Well, I'm here to explore change, the change to the make-up and character of a village that isn't just any old village, but that particular place that helped form me. And I have a particular angle on that change. As I walk towards the end of the string of little cottages I decide it was time to head back to the church.

My journey the 30 or so miles from my home in Poole to Stour Row rewinds a story. It is my story. But it is also a small piece of the story of the established church in this country. Seven years ago I had a call from my mother. She told me the news that the church in Stour Row had closed. This will not have come as a surprise to most of the village. But it was something of a surprise to me. More significantly, I was surprised at the sense of sadness and loss that it produced in me. I grieved a little for this village and for the church that had closed. A church I never attended.

Having come to faith in my late teens, I left deeply rural Stour Row for university and never returned. I find myself 30 years later living in a city and working as a Church of England minister, trying to enable the church to connect creatively with its changing context. I have generally had an eye for the future of the church. I have always sought to look over the horizon at the cultural landscape coming towards me and ask how the church needs to adapt to meet that world. I have rarely spared a thought for the past. I have seldom paid any attention to the rural church. It has not been my calling, and perhaps I've been guilty of that urban habit of assuming the future is always urban, and that the rural is a kind of cultural and technological backwater that will only change in the wake of the innovation created in the city. So what I felt when I heard the news of the closure of All Saints in Stour Row stirred me. It propelled me into a journey to listen and learn about the challenges of the rural church To widen my narrow lens on the future and include in its scope the stories of those responding to the challenge of being the church in places like Stour Row.[1]

In some small way, I am a witness to the trajectory of the church in the last 30 years, and a witness to some of the attempts to bring about its renewal. This has been my ministry, my experience, and the source of a great deal of reflection, study and personal investment. I want to tell something of that story. A story that feels like a small but significant perspective on a short but perhaps crucial chapter in the story of the church trying to find its way in the secular landscape of the UK. I invite you to take this journey with me. Within this story there are

---

[1] I interviewed a number of church leaders in the course of gathering these stories. Those interviewed are identified by name in the text. However other people referred to have been given pseudonyms.

folk struggling with the same challenges, seeking answers to the same questions, who also tell their stories and give their reflections.

This book is built around the journey from loss to hope, from death to resurrection, that is itself the shape of the gospel. This is surely the shape of the story we must inhabit as a church. 'Part 1: Lamentation' begins with the story of the death of a church and an examination of some of the realities of decline and frailty, but also creativity, in particular among some of our rural churches. 'Part 2: Waiting' reflects on some of my own experiences of church planting, which in recent years has become a key methodology for finding ways out of the crisis of decline. This part seeks to offer some reflections on both the promise and limitations of this approach. Finally, 'Part 3: Resurrection' reflects on networks of small, intentional missional communities that are emerging alongside our time-honoured churches. As I hope will become clear, I do not see this emerging movement as *the* substance of a resurrected church. It is one sign of a renewing movement emerging independently in all sorts of places as people seek to follow the *missio Dei*, God's Spirit of mission, at work in our communities.

Threading through the whole book is the theme of time. There is a great deal of anxiety and urgency within the church, which has been intensified by the impact of the Covid pandemic. Time, we feel, is running out for the church – at least as we know it. Yet crisis is not new. And time is not a thing that 'runs out'. It is a sacred element of creation through which God brings about his purposes, in God's time. Above all I hope this story places our sense of crisis and urgency within the wider context of the history of God's people, for whom crisis has never been far away, and for whom eternity and the grace of God's time have been a source of life and hope.

PART I

Lamentation

'The past is not dead, it's not even the past.'
William Faulkner

The Lighthouse – A Parable

There was once a lighthouse that stood on a cliff above the shore. It was an important lighthouse, warning ships away from danger. It had stood on the cliff for as long as anyone could remember. However, the cliff was starting to erode and fall into the sea.

Each winter, storms came and some of the cliff would be lost into the sea. And each year the storms got worse. And each year the edge of the cliff got closer to the lighthouse. So the people of the village got together and asked: 'What shall we do?! Soon the lighthouse will fall into the sea and the lighthouse will be lost and ships will not be safe.'

And some said: 'The lighthouse has always been here, it will be here for years to come. Don't worry!' And others said: 'We will move the lighthouse! Brick by brick back from the edge of the cliff.' And others said: 'The lighthouse wasn't built to last for ever! If you move the lighthouse it will only last a few more years before you have to move it again!'

But some posed a different question to the people: 'If we let the lighthouse fall into the sea, what other ways are there of doing its job of warning ships away from danger?' They argued that the storms were here to stay, the weather was getting worse, the erosion of the cliff was going to continue because the climate was changing.

The argument raged on in the village, some taking one position and others another. A group was started with the aim of strengthening the cliff and preserving the lighthouse in its present position. Another group started a fundraising campaign to move the lighthouse in from the edge of the cliff. And a small number began talking to the sailors and the fishermen, asking *them for creative solutions to the problem of how to know where the rocks are and how to avoid them. And the storms came and the cliff continued to fall into the sea, and the edge of the cliff continued to get closer to the lighthouse.*

I

All Saints, Stour Row, Dorset

My family were not religious, or Christian. We put Church of England on the census forms, but we were not churchgoers. For my part the church in our village was a total mystery. On Sunday mornings the lane filled up with a modest line of cars that stretched down towards our house. We knew one set of neighbours who went, but they didn't seem to talk much about their church involvement. My only connection with the church in all the time I was growing up came one Christmas when

I was asked to play the flute for a Christmas concert. A lady who dwelt in one of the cottages down the lane turned out to be the occasional organist at the church and asked me to play, which I reluctantly accepted. Apart from that the church was a black box in which things certainly happened, which a small minority of the village engaged with (though quite who I was never sure).

My father knew the vicar a little. He was a regular at the pub in the next village which was my father's favourite destination for a lunchtime beer. My father used to joke that the local vicar spent more time in the public bar of the pub than in his churches. It was probably true, but then that was also true for most of the population of the various villages in his parish, so who could blame him? That would have been the best way to get to know them. At the time I had no conception of what a vicar stood for. This vicar was something of an eccentric character, ranting about the state of the church ('It's not the diocese's church, it's Christ's church!') to anyone who would listen.

Not long before we arrived in Stour Row, the pub closed. The College Arms was now a house called, inevitably, The Old College Arms. In the early years of our time there the village had a garage, a shop, the village hall and the church. The garage closed a few years in. The shop not long after. We had lived through the beginnings of that pattern, now familiar everywhere, of the decline of villages such as ours, as initially supermarkets and more latterly online shopping decimated local economies. The social capital of the village was maintained for many years by the village hall and the church. But somehow, even as I was growing up, there was a sense that the fabric of village life was unravelling a bit with the loss of these things. People met less often without the happenstance afforded by chance meetings at the village shop. So even though the church had little relevance in my life growing up in this village, news of its closure felt like the final act in the long slow death of a village.

Back on my return visit to Stour Row I walk up the lane past my old family home and approach the closed church of All Saints. Over the low stone wall between the lane and the churchyard it's immediately obvious that nature is beginning to take over. The grass around the older gravestones is still being cut, but around the side and back of the church a wilderness has developed. Through the gate a gravel path running up to the door of the church can still just be discerned. However, a thick scattering of cowslips now festoons the approach. To the left of the gate I stop at what could perhaps be called our family burial ground. A bit of a grand term for what I now find to be three pronounced indentations in the turf under which some excavation and weed clearance reveal the memorial stones of my sister, my grandmother and my father. It's strange seeing these markers in this place for some of the most significant people in my life. For my sister, who hardly lived here because she spent most of our time in this village living in a specialist care facility in Dorchester. For my grandmother, who lived most of her life near Oxford and died after a short spell in a nursing home in Shaftesbury. For my father, who had lived here for perhaps 15 years of his nearly 90-year life. I guess there are some places that take on a significance and an identity from the intensity of the formation that takes place in them. This is where our family took its shape and where others embraced us. For all its insignificance now, a few ribbons of undistinguished houses lying in the lea of a hill in north Dorset, Stour Row remains our place. And so the churchyard becomes some kind of place of pilgrimage, even for this family for whom entering the gate into the churchyard always proved something of a daring venture.

I begin to move around and tour the other memorials and headstones, reading familiar names, neighbours, well-known farming families. The graveyard is closed to new burials now. Much of it is sinking into that unregimented look of old headstones perched at odd angles. Among them, though, is a relatively new grave. It is the grave of Gordon Ralph. On the headstone are inscribed the words 'Farmer of this Parish'. The Ralphs are a longstanding farming family from the village. Their land was visible from our back garden. Monday evenings in the summer months would sometimes be punctuated by the plaintive lowing of cows from the Ralphs' farm, cows whose calves had been taken to the nearby market at Sturminster Newton that day. The Ralphs hosted the village fete in their garden each year. Most years my father ran the 'whisky draw' – a simple tombola affair with a bottle of mediocre whisky as a prize. And most years, despite my attempts at finding an excuse, I was roped in to help. This was the village fete where the most popular event involved people placing bets on a grid representing the field beyond the Ralphs' garden. At a given time in the afternoon the Ralphs' herd of dairy cows were released from the shade of the barn into the field and everyone gathered to watch, their grid reference in hand. The winner was the owner of the square on which the first cow emptied its bowels.

So Gordon Ralph had died. He had remained in my memory as a fit, not particularly old man, who gave off an easy confidence not uncommon for someone who has known his place in the world all his life and is well practised at inhabiting it. I mentally added 30 years of age to this frozen image and, of course, it made sense.

The Ralphs were village royalty in a way. Part of the furniture without which the village didn't function – parish, fete, village hall, WI – they and others like them held the place together. There was every possibility that another generation of Ralphs had risen to take Gordon's place. And yet with the church closed, the gravestones drooping into the ground and the cowslips rising to take over, Gordon's gravestone and its particularly poignant inscription seemed something of a final word. Because farming and parish just went together in a way that is increasingly no longer the case. Gordon Ralph represented that deep relationship in the history of Anglicanism, and in English culture certainly, between the Christian faith and the land, between the church and place. 'A threefold cord of soul, soil and society' as Andrew Rumsey lyrically describes it.[1] Parish is not simply an expression of geography. It represents something far deeper, far more profound: a signifier of Gordon Ralph and his family's deep belonging to and identification with this place, its people and the faith that is part of that whole tradition, holding land, people and life together. Farmer, of this parish.

So I suppose I was – am – 'of this parish'. And though I was oblivious at the time, the various vicars of our era here thought so too. And others since have seen it that way, enough anyway to provide space for my relatives to find their place in the church's burial ground. But what does it mean now for this place to be a parish? As the strands of social and spiritual capital increasingly unravel in villages like Stour Row, as villages like ours increasingly become places for leisurely retirement, a retreat from the world, rather than places of working and community life, as villages fight to retain the social and commercial hubs, including churches, that define village life, what does it mean for the church to see them as parishes? What is the future of the church in a village like Stour Row, where the church's life and identity have been so intricately bound up with a world that is disappearing?

✠

I turn the car around, a rather embarrassing five-point turn in my beast of car, and head reluctantly out of Stour Row. I am driving through the Benefice of the Stour Vale churches which, though not now including Stour Row, contains seven parish churches all looked after by one vicar. Multi-parish benefices are the standard parish arrangement these days, a common response to the reality of falling attendances meaning that more and more small congregations are needed to fund a single stipendiary vicar. Seven parishes is a lot, but there are benefices with far more. In Lincolnshire there is a benefice with 27 parishes.

There is a sense of a new phase, a new time, in the life of the parish system. Decline is not new, as anyone with half an eye on the relevant statistics will know. But a more feverish anxiety about the potential collapse of the whole system seems to have emerged as we have moved beyond the intense challenges of the Covid lockdowns. Research by the Evangelical Alliance suggests that the pandemic has caused a significant shift in patterns of attendance across the church. As a rule of thumb it suggests that a third of people have gone back as normal, a third have gone back but are not giving as much of their time to enabling congregations to function, and a third have yet to come back (and may not come back at all).[2] Of course it can easily be said that it's still too early to draw conclusions of any certainty. Many are still concerned to return to in-person worship and many churches continue to offer both in-person and livestreamed services. So it may be too early to say. But I think it's fair to say that something has shifted significantly. A shift that is consistent with patterns that were emerging before the pandemic accelerated them.

In Scotland, Steve Aisthorpe's research into church leavers suggests that as many as a third of committed churchgoers have left churches in which they were previously highly engaged. A common argument is that such people have become less committed in their faith. However, Aisthorpe's work tells a different story. His research suggests that those who have left have done so in order to *better pursue their faith*. They are tired of church having little engagement with their communities and tired of working hard to deliver weekly services and church programmes for the congregation. And they are often disenchanted with a church that doesn't seem to offer space to question, to doubt and to explore things more deeply. They want a practised faith that engages with the experience of their practical lives, their work, their communities, the issues in the world around.[3] To be fair, this is unlikely to be the main reason why All Saints, Stour Row had to close. The age profile of the congregation, even when I was growing up in the village, does not fit that of the research cohort Aisthorpe was exploring. But it does signal that there are other forces at work that are powering decline and intensifying the conversation about the future of the church.

I am driving to see the vicar of the Stour Vale Churches who has agreed for me to have a conversation with him and his wife about All Saints and the present ministry in his parish. I drive round the side of Duncliffe Wood, the hill on whose gentle slopes Stour Row sits, through East Stour, over the river into West Stour and then down the next hill and into Kington Magna. In years gone by, as the common mythology goes, each village had its vicar, who was part of the village community, drifting around on a bike, making pastoral visits, acting as a focal point and rallying point for the life of the parish. James K. Smith remarks that 'the most significant problem with nostalgia is not what it remembers but what it forgets.'[4] Indeed, All Saints Church never had its own vicar in the neat simple sense that many might imagine. As the village of Stour Row developed in the 1700s it became part of a parish that included two neighbouring villages, Todber and Stour Provost. The three villages were served by one vicar, a fact not lost on those presently serving the benefice. For many years people from the village of Stour Row would make their way to church along the old drove road to Stour Provost. It wasn't until 1867 that money was raised for a church building at Stour Row. All Saints was officially opened as a Chapel of Ease in 1868.[5]

I reflect on that phrase 'Chapel of Ease' as I drive the five and a half miles to the house of the current vicar. It's a phrase that demonstrates the simple ecclesiology of a time that has passed, where the development of a new settlement would bring calls for the founding of a new church building to enable those who lived there to worship together without the need for long journeys. I think about what it might mean to build a 'chapel of ease' today. The concept of making it easier for people to come to church remains a powerful driver. Behind it lies the assumption that there is still a residual default in the general population that churchgoing is something they would do if the circumstances were made sufficiently easy. Decline can surely be addressed by making our services more accessible, more relevant to a younger generation, by adapting our ancient buildings to be more welcoming, more visible, by modernizing the style of music we use, the style of dress ...

There was certainly nothing inaccessible about the church of All Saints when I was growing up in the village. I could roll out of bed and be there at the door of the church in about three minutes if I was really inclined. It could have been my very own Chapel of Ease if I had wanted it to be. However, what took place within that building was simply mysterious and alien to me. I had no conception of who went or what they did. More significantly, there was nothing in the wider life of the village that could have told me anything about the life of this group of people who parked their cars on our lane on a Sunday morning and walked up that now overgrown path to the church. There were no clues laid out that could have told me that what took place in that building had some kind of connection with my life or that of my parents. It is that experience, for me growing up there and perhaps for others in the village, that might well have sown the seeds of the demise of All Saints. The little congregation that met there seemed to exist in a different world. They came and they went for a few hours a week. The rest of the week the church lay dormant and silent, surrounded by graves. The church was easy to ignore. It was certainly not easy to access. There was nothing that the church congregation did, no human or social interface other than what happened inside the walls on a Sunday morning, that gave me any invitation to access the world they inhabited.

I drive up the long and narrow lane from the main road towards the little village of Kington Magna and find my way to the house belonging to Richard, the Vicar of the Stour Vale Benefice. We are joined by his wife Barbara who is currently in training to be a licensed lay minister. Together we piece together the story of the closure of All Saints. This seems to have come down to a competition for scarce resources to run both the church and the village hall. A public meeting had been convened by the vicar at the time calling for help to run the church, without which it would close. At the meeting some certainly expressed a great concern for the life of the village if the church closed. But when it came down to it no-one came forward to fill the offices of the church needed to run it. Barbara tells me, 'Both the village hall and the church were sort of fighting for help from the same pool of people. And eventually the village hall won.'

Scarcity of resources to do the considerable amount of work needed to run small congregations that meet in old and often listed buildings is clearly a common issue for benefices like Stour Vale. Richard tells me that most of his churchwardens, those with local responsibility for the care of the building, are over 80. 'And I'm sorry,' he says, 'but when you get to 80 you really don't want to take on a churchwarden's job. But there is nobody else.' 'We're reliant all the time on a very small pool of people who've always done it and are still enthusiastic about doing it', Barbara says. 'But in a lot of cases, it's "the spirit is willing, but the flesh is weak." You know, they're tired. I think the challenge is finding those people to come up and step up to the plate and be the future really.' Barbara tells me that as part of her training for licensed ministry in the benefice she explored the closure of the church at Stour Row, the reasons for it and its impact on the village. She spent time interviewing residents in the village about how they felt the closure of the church had affected the village. 'Four years later,' Barbara says, 'the loss of All Saints seems to have created little significance for the village.' Two of those that Barbara interviewed when asked what effect the church's closure had had on life the village responded bluntly 'none'.[6] Barbara's reflections on the church's closure typify the complex dilemmas that many such village churches face. They may well recognize that churches have lost a living connection with their community. They may recognize the need to see the church as more than the building. Yet the building provides something without which the life of the church community seems to struggle. Equally, the demands of the building are a drain on the energy and time needed to engage more widely in the life of the village.

This makes me think that surely Stour Row is not an outlier. I know the character of the villages of the Stour Vale to be quite similar. Sure, some are prettier than others, some slightly smaller and others bigger. Indeed, Stour Row with a population of 300 is if anything one of the larger villages. But all share a similar farming heritage and all have seen a similar process of change, particularly in recent decades. Those with links to the traditional farming origins of these villages have dwindled and they have become desirable places for people from the cities to retire. Barbara reckons there is only one person left in Stour Row who can trace their family back generations to the time the church was built in 1878. Richard reflects that many moving into the villages now are people retiring early from the military and business. The average price of a house in Kington Magna is £450,000.

So I ask the inevitable question regarding how many of Richard's seven churches might be under threat of closure in the near future. 'I would say,' Richard replies, 'at least two of my churches, and it could be as high as four, could be gone within the next two to three years.' I'm surprised at Richard's candour. He is by no means someone wearied by the demands of rural ministry. He still enjoys it. Still finds it a great privilege and still finds moments of reward and hope in the opportunities afforded by being a parish priest. He refers to the 'tremendous amount of good will' that he experiences and the generosity and grace extended to him and others by those in his congregations. 'We've still got fairly good numbers and people that are willing to do the work. If we go another five years, and I do say as little as five years, I wonder whether we will be still in that position, or will we have lost so many people that actually we can't recover?'

I leave Kington Magna and start to head east toward Shaftesbury to visit my mother who now lives there. I pass three of

Richard's churches on that journey and it is hard to escape the cultural significance of these buildings that mark the landscape and provide such a focus for each of these villages, and of course for thousands more like them. It's almost a cliché to say that the church is not the building. That truth is asserted by some as though people in rural villages are thoroughly unaware of it. And yes, there is certain amount of idolatry, or 'folk religion' as Richard called it, that elevates the building to a level that Christian doctrine, and Anglican ecclesiology, do not warrant. There remains a traditionalist belligerence in some places that means that the very idea of travelling a few miles to a neighbouring village to attend a very similar service to one that might have taken place closer to home, can't be embraced. As Richard said, 'We've got two parishes next door to each other. They are about a mile and a half apart. They will not set foot in each other's churches.'

So certainly that attitude exists and it's not uncommon. And it might be tempting to argue therefore that the problem is precisely in the buildings themselves. Buildings that are immobile, sometimes in the wrong place, expensive to heat and maintain and lacking in basic amenities. Making the kind of alterations and developments that might open them up to a greater variety of uses in the life of these villages is both complex and expensive. But doing away with them is not the silver bullet. A deliberate policy of church closure may save a great deal of money in the immediate future, but what does it do for the witness of the church in that place? As Richard argued: 'If you look at the Methodist Church, what Methodist Church? URC? What URC? They've all pulled in and in and in and eventually there's nothing.'

I think of All Saints again. It's easy to project, but there was undoubtedly a feeling for me, even as someone who doesn't get very excited by church buildings, that the soul of the building had gone. It soon becomes very clear that a closed or abandoned church building has lost its heart when the congregation vacates. And as much as the church is indeed the people, we return to the sense that it is more than just people. It is people who are part of living tradition, for which this building in this place, with its unbroken thread to the village's origins and its generations of people, holds this story in some important kind of way. And in turn this story, this conversation between people and place and certain particular buildings, is wrapped up in the greater story of the gospel, of the life, death and resurrection of Jesus and his living presence in the lives of people in particular places throughout the generations. Yes, this story does not *require* a building. And yes, at times you might think that some people have swapped Jesus for architectural heritage as the heart of the story. Yet it's hard to escape just what an important gathering, sustaining, shaping role these buildings have in the ongoing life of the Christian communities in these, and indeed in any places.

Notes

1 Rumsey, *Parish*, p. 157.
2 https://www.eauk.org/assets/files/downloads/Changing-Church-Autumn-2021-Research-Report.pdf (accessed 8.2.2024). Research conducted around the same time (October 2021) by the Church of England shows a 29% decline in average all-age weekly attendance since before the pandemic: https://www.churchofengland.org/media-and-news/press-releases/statistics-mission-2021-published (accessed 8.2.24).
3 Aisthorpe, *The Invisible Church*.
4 Smith, *How To Inhabit Time*, p. 38.
5 Jordan, *A History of Stour Row*.
6 Priest, 'Gone ... and Almost Forgotten'. An essay assignment generously given to me by email.

2

St Catherine's Chapel, Milton Abbas, Dorset

There are still places where a prayer speaks itself.
Where the door opens on a space
Full of nothing but the gift of attention.
Where the rising track through the beechwood
Arrives at a clearing in the soul,
Like a transept in the structure of creation,
A place where prayer is as simple as an acorn,
As formed as the heart silenced.

It's the start of another year and I am taking a long walk, to pray and reflect before the year draws me into its busyness. I have heard of St Catherine's Chapel but never visited. It is hidden in the woods above Milton Abbey, just beyond the village of Milton Abbas. Walking along the road from the village you pass under a bridge that carries an old track between the Abbey and the Chapel. To access the chapel a path traverses the hill from further on. The path is cluttered with fallen trees and branches, a devastation created by the latest alphabetized storm to sweep through. I pick my way steadily to the twelfth-century building through dense stands of beech.

The chapel is a simple rectangular building orientated in line with the Abbey. A bench at its west end gives a clear view down the slope and on to the Abbey in the valley below. For six centuries from the late tenth century a Benedictine community lived and worshipped there. Milton Abbas grew as a market town in the shadow of this significant monastic community whose life came to an abrupt end in 1539 with the dissolution of the monasteries under Henry VIII. Since then it has been a private estate, a healing centre and latterly a private school. The church, however, still plays a part in the life of the place and recently a new expression of Benedictine life has formed, a dispersed community of prayer inspired by the Benedictine tradition and centred on the Abbey.

From the chapel I descend to the road again and climb the bridleway toward Bulbarrow Hill. It's heavy going underfoot after so much rain in the past few weeks. More branches have been cleared from the path, their neatly severed ends suggesting the hasty work of chainsaws to make the path accessible. Rotting wood is everywhere, slowly recycling materials into the earth through the work of huge numbers of insects and fungi – an encouraging sign of the renewed appreciation of the critical importance of death and decay to the ecosystem of a wood.

One particular rotting ash tree catches my eye. Its branches are lined with round black knobs of something that looks like a conker. A sharp twist on one of them and the 'conker' comes off in my hand. It is the fungus commonly known as King Alfred's

Cakes and I know it for its use in bushcraft. When dried it can be cut to reveal wood-like material inside, with rings of growth like a tree. This surface will hold a spark in a tinder box. In theory you can throw a spark onto a piece of King Alfred's Cake, or place a small ember from a previous fire on its surface, and carry the spark through to the end of the day when you might need to light a fire again.

I walk up through the woods and out onto the gentler, higher slopes of Bulbarrow until I reach the escarpment and the view over the Blackmoor Vale. Buzzards are circling and arcing fast on the sharp north wind. I don't stay long, returning on a different bridleway down through the woods to the south. I stop to rest on a sunny slope sheltered from the wind. Above the tops of the beech trees chattering fieldfares rush past in small intermittent flocks. Sitting on the stump of a felled tree I am again aware of the sheer volume of forest matter strewn around and left to rot into the soil.

Death and decay are such a critical part of the life of an ecosystem. But the deepening appreciation of the richness of this phase of life is revealing. Instead of seeing death and decay as a difficult but necessary conduit to new life in the future, simply the recycling of organic material, it is increasingly being understood how much death and decay are a critical part of the ecosystem's very present life. Death and decay are intrinsic generative elements of the whole system, providing habitats for species that the ecosystem cannot do without.

I think of the Abbey again. Protestantism since the Reformation, when the Abbey was dissolved, has struggled to find space for the generative life offered by the monastic movements. These movements spinning off from the edges of the traditional church have historically been sources of renewal for the church over time. And now the church that Henry VIII bullied into existence is decaying, across Dorset and across the country.

The answer to the challenge of decline is not simple, despite the protestations of certain movements who will tell you that simply this or that needs to happen. Something much bigger is happening. Something akin to the cultural upheaval of the

Reformation which swept nations into its orbit in the sixteenth century. Call it what you like: secularism, liberalism, consumer-capitalism, the age of individual expression – the net effect is a marginalization of the church and the faith it is founded on.

In such times the Christian faith has often found the spark for its future in the small and communal movements of Christian life that emerge on the edges of the institution. It was the Benedictine movement that was credited with incubating the Christian faith through the Dark Ages and into an era of flourishing Christian spirituality in the medieval age.

I take the small black coal of the King Alfred's Cake from my pocket, a spore-bearing body drawn from the slow death of a part of this wood. And I wonder if it is not the small, the communal, the prayerful and the simple expressions of Christian faith to which we might turn to find hope for the future in a secular age? Are these the sparks that will carry the Christian life and hope from the decay of the present to light the fires of the future?

☩

A few months later I drive north, up the course of the river Stour below Blandford Forum and then left and over the hill into the Winterborne Valley. These places hold an important place in my own story. I came to faith at school and went to church intermittently at a small independent church in Blandford. I was welcomed in by a family who were founding members of the church and whose daughters both went to the same school as me. It was a church that had been part of the house church movement of the 1970s, rediscovering the simplicity of church based on small tight-knit groups of people, dispensing with the need for a building and meeting in their own homes. By the time I started attending from time to time the community had grown and taken use of a building in the town of Blandford. Occasional Sundays in those early days of faith would involve a morning service followed by lunch at the farm in Winterborne

ST CATHERINE'S CHAPEL, MILTON ABBAS, DORSET

Stickland and then at some point the journey home, over Bulbarrow Hill and back through the lanes to Stour Row.

The road takes me down the hill and into the village of Winterborne Stickland with its long street of cottages flanking the stream that emerges from the dip slope of the chalk ridge of Bulbarrow. It's a seasonal stream, hence winter-borne, drying up in summer as the porous chalk soaks up the limited rain and re-emerging in winter when the ground starts to saturate. The result of this and the consequent settlement of the valley in which the stream runs is a long thin benefice of parishes running from Turnworth at one end to Winterborne Whitechurch at the other. To this in recent years has been added the parish of Milton Abbas, with its stunning street of matching whitewashed thatch cottages running up the hill from the estate that contains the Abbey. Its old, but most clearly planned, look is no coincidence. When the Abbey estate came into the hands of Joseph Damer in 1752 he set about the hugely ambitious project of reshaping the whole estate and building a grand house in the grounds of the Abbey. The project included the gradual destruction and replacement of the houses that formed Middleton, a town clustered around the Abbey. By 1779 Damer had razed each of these dwellings to the ground and completed the construction of the street of identical cottages some half a mile distant, further away and most definitely out of sight of his new manor house.

Places are shaped by a variety of forces; geographical, political, cultural, happenstance, the sheer will of human beings to make their mark on a place. The peace of the wooded valley that contains Milton Abbas was as much an attraction for Benedictine monks seeking a place of prayer as it was for Joseph Damer seeking a place of tranquillity for his dream house. In a strange way that spiritual deposit of place-making, formed by centuries of a monastic community here, remains as a number of footholds on the map. The Abbey itself remains the property of the local diocese, its thresholds a legal boundary between it and the jurisdiction of the private school that now occupies Damer's grand house. Meanwhile a similar legal distinction exists along the foundations and lintels of St Catherine's chapel in the woods above the Abbey, demarcating the lines of responsibility between the Forestry Commission and the diocese. Are these residual islands of ecclesial property simply an administrative and historic burden? Are we just becoming a kind of ecclesiastical wing of the National Trust? Or do such places hold within them the memory, the living tradition, the sparks of another chapter in the spiritual life of people here?

✣

I arrive to have a conversation with Lewis, the vicar of the benefice. He had arrived in the middle of the first of the Covid lockdowns, meeting his parishioners all together on Zoom with all the buildings closed. Lewis admits that those early services on Zoom were a delight for many people. Suddenly, dispersed congregations, each a handful knocking around in an old building, were a community of 50 people sharing together online. Lewis has six churches all within a roughly three-mile radius of the vicarage. It's not difficult to make a case for closing perhaps half of these and gathering these small congregations into something a bit more substantial. Yet every village is different. Each has its own unique history and personality. Each building its own signature associated with its particular village.

As things opened up after lockdown, and as many who hadn't accessed Zoom started to feel able to attend their local church again, it proved impossible to hold on to the sense of being a community across the whole benefice. However, it's clear that, although a sense of being one community across these small villages was positive, Lewis believes in the importance of ancient church buildings for the life of these communities. 'The buildings have a ministry,' he says. One of the first things he had done when it became possible, with Covid restrictions loosening, was to ensure that each of his buildings could be made open. Automatic locks now open and close the churches each day so that anyone passing can go in, a neat solution to the challenge of finding someone willing and available to physically unlock and lock these places.

'The buildings have a ministry.' A nice phrase. One that touches on the reality for many people that these spaces, precious and distinctive, still have the power to enable a quality of reflection and even transcendent experience. But it's a phrase that can be overplayed. The 'ministry' of these buildings is not a function of a particular configuration of stonework in a particular place. Like Damer's resituated village, you can't just make a new village and call it a community. The ministry of these buildings is a function of a living tradition of people and place, the particular narrative of incarnational life unfurling in a place, written into the fabric of the building. As though to illustrate this, Lewis tells me of the developing story of two of his buildings.

Winterborne Clenston is a beautiful, spired church in resplendent isolation on the road south of Winterborne Stickland. There is no apparent reason for a church to be there. Until you learn that a number of villages used to exist here but declined into obscurity around the time of the Black Death. Buildings have long memories. The church at Clenston has been maintained and kept alive by generations of gentry. The current Patron of two of the villages in the benefice now funds its upkeep. A church that hosts one traditional service each month, attended by a handful of people who are regulars at some of the other churches in the benefice, is perhaps the most beautifully appointed, equipped and maintained of any in the area. In one sense then there is no future for a church like this. It doesn't have a worshipping community in the standard sense. It has a smattering of loyal folk who will drive a few miles for a particular service in a beautiful building. It only exists through the largesse of a local landowner. Yet for Lewis there is a sense that the benefice can hold this space as a place of pilgrimage and prayer. People come here, park their cars, walk the gently rolling hills of the surrounding countryside and almost without fail enter the church for a visit. 'How do we create this place or facilitate it as a prayerful space?' Lewis asks, 'What resources can we put into that? Are there opportunities for churches or groups to use it for retreat days and places, because it's beautifully cared for?' Maybe such a place can have a ministry, not just to the few who attend each month but to a host of other people beyond the community of these little villages who will find in this space a place of silence and retreat in the peace of this rural Dorset valley.

On a spur of the Winterborne valley, just a mile from Winterborne Stickland, is the tiny village of Winterborne Houghton. Lewis tells me that on his arrival in the benefice he had a call to tell him that the church was now in the situation of having no churchwarden and no treasurer. Like Richard in the Stour Vale, the struggle to find people to fill the voluntary posts that make the life of a parish church possible is perhaps the key thing that threatens these churches with closure. Lewis suggested that the church take a year to consider its future and whether it should close. The option of making the church a 'festival church' – that is, opening only for the high days and holidays, Christmas, Easter and so on – was mooted. However, as things opened up after Covid, a small group of regular worshippers began to explore a different approach.

The church at Houghton is up on the side of the narrow valley, set in a large churchyard from which you can look up the valley and down over the cottages of the village. It is a beautiful spot with a sense of being part of nature at the same time as being part of the village. With people still reluctant or unable to meet in the church building, the little group at Houghton decided that the churchyard was actually an asset and a good place to meet. The group began to organize gatherings for worship in the churchyard. Major festivals were celebrated in the churchyard, likewise pet services and harvest services. They installed creative displays that engaged anyone walking past. And what has changed is not that the church community is suddenly thriving but that the boundaries between village and church have become more porous, the church community more outward facing, more engaged in its community, more attentive to the connections that might be made with the Christian tradition and the ongoing life of the village. 'There were four people there who were committed to their village, saying how do we make this church be at the centre of community life?"' Lewis explains: 'So it was messy and still is messy, but it kind of works.' The church remains without a churchwarden or a treasurer; instead 'we have four people on the PCC, who are already good friends. And it's relational and multigenerational [and] they all live next door to each other. And so more than any PCC, it functions better. Because they are "Well, we will do this bit if you do that bit", then they tell me what's going on.'

There is something in this story that seems to tilt the dilemma of the future of these buildings at a different angle. It changes the question. Not how can we keep this building and its worshipping life going? But how can this building serve and shape the life of this community? And how can it do so in a way that is clearly connected with the Christian story that has been sustained by this building and its people for generations? Buildings then become not the focus but the facilitator of something more engaged, more outward facing, more future oriented. So much of our perspective on these buildings often appears woefully nostalgic, rehearsing visions of a time when they were full, even though it's doubtful they ever were. They fixate on a building's history as a static thing rather than as one part of a living story that may yet have power to open another chapter in the future.

☩

Nostalgia is a powerful draw in these times of decline, bending us backwards and inwards to images of the past as beacons for the future. Ilya Prigogine was a Nobel prize-winning chemist whose work opened up the scientific community to the world of chaos and emergence. Prigogine spent his whole scientific life exploring reality from the perspective of the irreversibility of time. Time does not reverse, it only goes forward. You cannot step in the same river twice. There is a contingency and emergent reality written into creation. Nostalgia, said Prigogine, 'is the substitution of real time for imaginary time'.[1] Living in the contingency of irreversible time means that living in the present is both a product of the memory of the past and also a reflection of our hopes for the future. We live in what German philosopher Edmund Husserl called a 'temporal halo', a consciousness in time which is a conversation between a past retained and a future anticipated. If this is true for individuals it is also true for communities. 'Each collective', says James K. Smith, 'has its temporal halo'.[2]

The true meaning of nostalgia does indeed harbour this more nuanced consciousness of our place in time. Nostalgia means 'a longing for home'. It is the expressed desire we have for something that is beyond our memories of the past and our current experience, yet something we long for and which, we sense, we might recognize should we see it. Time is linear, irreversible, as Prigogine realized in a profound way. And yet time is also circular. It moves forward as a conversation between the past, present and future such that our conception and experience of life deepens in recognition and understanding. In the first of T. S. Eliot's Four Quartets the linearity of time is questioned. Present and past are bound up in the future. Our lives, lived in time's arrow, nevertheless bend and circle in time such that an ending is so often a beginning. We journey through time and yet return home 'and know the place for the first time'.[3] What we thought of as home, as base, as origin, becomes new, becomes novel, by virtue of a richer resonance with the truth of what it was always meant to be.

Some weeks after my visit to Lewis for our conversation, we meet at St Catherine's Chapel. As we park up at the farm shop nearby, we bump into the vicar of the next-door parish. He and others have just come from a service of prayer in the chapel, part of the rhythm of prayer of the new Benedictine community that has sprung up in the past few years. Lewis and I start the walk up the gentle slope through the wood of mature beech trees on the hillside overlooking the Abbey. Lewis describes the service that takes place here every Christmas. The route is lit by lanterns and the congregation likewise carry lanterns as they follow the route toward the small barn-like chapel in a clearing of the wood. I'm not surprised to hear that with little or no advertising this service proves to be one of the most popular services of the whole year in the benefice.

We arrive at the Chapel, Lewis taking out the most enormous iron key to open up the large oak door on its south side. He wishes the Chapel could be open access, but has done his best by making a key available at the farm shop. Inside, the simplicity and the silence is deeply affecting. The chancel has an uneven tiled floor, with long wooden pews lining the walls; a narrow entrance at one end leads to a small sanctuary with a plain stone altar. A large iron candelabra hangs from the ceiling above the chancel, with melted stubs poking from the sockets. There is no natural light save for that entering through the door we came in.

Is it fanciful to say that such a place still holds the memory, the imprint, of centuries of prayers? Or to wonder at such a place being preserved as a sacred space, generations after the organized work of the monastery came to an end in the sixteenth century? It simply feels like a place to pray, a place that welcomes prayers, stillness, attentiveness. A place that invites a reception to the presence of God. And so perhaps it is not surprising that in Lewis's creative venturing towards the future for the benefice, he imagines this chapel as a locus for a prayerful community across the whole benefice. 'We have a number of people who are passionate about the church across the villages. And they're passionate about each other's churches as well and the ministry of the benefice. So what does it mean to have a group of individuals who underpin the life of all the parishes in prayer and community life in a depth that we can't do as six separate entities trying to keep the show on the road for good or for ill? What does a deep prayerful community look like where ideas can bubble up or maybe we can start to reimagine what parish life might look like? Maybe for rural multi-parish benefices there is a sense in which some kind of missional community might not replace what's going on, but underpin and be the scaffolding for some existing things, and perhaps some new things as well.'

This reimagining towards the future, a kind of living tradition that draws on the past and holds it lightly enough to allow it to shape the future, navigates us away from classic nostalgia. It accepts the irreversibility of time and embraces the circularity of time, the unfolding, disclosing nature of the ongoing story of the gospel through the life of the church in these places. But I am under no illusion from my conversation with Lewis just how difficult it is to navigate this dialectic path. Closure is a reality for some of his parishes, he admits, within the next few years. 'Most churches are living beyond their means. I think that will come to a head, and I think everyone sees it on the horizon in the next year, or year or two.' Part of the reality is also the sustainability or otherwise of the role of the vicar of the benefice itself.

Holding together the ministry of six parishes, the administration of the buildings, the classic ministry of weddings, funerals, Sunday services, the sheer weight of that responsibility in terms of time and organization, against the space and energy needed to creatively explore the future, is almost impossible. 'For me, one of the biggest things is just the pressure of day-to-day ministering and the things that come across my desk in terms of the good everyday ministry of the Church of England. But that's all-encompassing. To create a space to think and to have these kinds of conversations is almost impossible with six parishes. And maybe I always thought I could do that. But to some degree, I wonder how possible it is?' But in addition to the sheer weight of responsibility, the precariousness of posts like Lewis's also mitigates against the kind of energy and long-term vision needed to find a way into the future. In the background for Lewis there are conversations about new parish mergers, the development of an even bigger benefice that might be able to sustain a stipendiary minister. These conversations await the resignation of a local colleague and the opportunity for reorganization that that will enable. Meanwhile, in the present, giving the energy toward the future within the foreshadowing of these conversations is difficult. Lewis admits: 'It's very hard to develop ideas and plans. How much energy and vision do you put into developing stuff, and its sustainability, knowing that this kind of conversation is happening?'

┼

I take the unheralded turning to Winterbourne Houghton, wander about the churchyard and poke around in the open church. From a cherry tree not far from the west end of the church coloured ribbons hang, remnants of a recent churchyard service, signs of life. Inside, the standard furnishings of a parish country church are overlaid with signs of innovation, of the worshipping community hosting the village, blurring the stone and flint boundaries that have stood for centuries and which our secular age seem to have hardened. Like the library at the back, which stocks books both Christian and 'secular'. Hilary Mantel's *The Mirror and the Light* is among them. A reminder that cultural and religious upheaval is not exactly new in this or any other parish.

Driving back through Stickland and southwards along the route of the vanished chalk stream, the gentle dip-slope of this chalk landscape in the lea of Bulbarrow tips me down to the church at Clenston, beautiful in its untethered isolation. Place marker for a disappeared village.

Appearances and disappearances. Village and churches. Decline and renewal. Some churches may well wait out the drought with the promise of draughts of money from the deep wells of heritage and land. Others, though, must reimagine, make use of their assets in new ways, turn a cherry tree into a place of prayer, a bell tower into a library.

Notes

1 Quoted in an interview he gave which can be found at https://www.youtube.com/watch?v=2NCdpMlYJxQ (accessed 8.2.24).
2 Smith, *How To Inhabit Time*, pp. 29–31.
3 Eliot, *Four Quartets*.

3

St Mary's, Drimpton, Beaminster Team Ministry

A few weeks after my visit to Lewis I head westward, with the sea emerging sporadically between the hills and cliffs of the Jurassic coast. At Bridport I head north and up the narrowing valley that brings me into the town of Beaminster. The market square hosts the usual fare of local shops plus a sprinkling of boutique businesses with window displays lifted from a *Country Living* magazine. This is a stunning part of Dorset in which to live; remote, quiet, unspoilt and seemingly resistant to the creep of urban progress and development that touches many rural areas. I park in a narrow lane and find the parish church perched on a rise behind the market square, as though squeezed in as close as possible to the life of the town while trying hard not to intrude.

For over 10 years David, the Rector of the Beaminster Team, and Jo the Pioneer Priest, have been conducting a brave experiment in parish ministry. David possesses with conviction a vision for the renewal of the Christian faith in Beaminster and the surrounding villages which begins with doing something different. And which begins elsewhere. It begins with the forging of new relationships and the offering of new ways of engaging with the Christian faith. At the same time the regular members of the 13 existing churches in the benefice have been assured that the traditional ministry of the parish will be maintained. As David puts it: 'I think it's an understanding that things can be done differently. So long as, and the trade-off is, you keep some of the traditional going as well.'

I enter the cool and generous space of the church, where Jo is clearing away the boxes of plastic toys and other paraphernalia from the weekly toddler group. The spaces behind the pulpit and under the communion table provide a convenient way to conceal it all in readiness for a communion service later in the week. It strikes me that the unseen presence of these items in the church as the inherited liturgy is performed once again is perhaps a good metaphor for the uneasy relationship between all that Jo has been developing over the years alongside the ongoing life of the traditional parish church.

☩

The question raised, as I help conceal toddler group materials under the high altar, is whether these two strands can co-exist? Will the renewing stream of life brought into being by the work of a pioneer find its way into the traditional? Or will it find its own rhythm and its own emerging tradition, faithful to the old but distinct from it? These questions reach into the heart of the matter of how we imagine the future of the church: not just the rural church, but the whole church. What is our vision, our theory (and theology) of change? Margaret Wheatley and Deborah Frieze have described a process of change that sees the emergence of a new system of operation in a given field, separate from the old as the old declines. They point to a gap between the declining curve of one system and the emerging upcurve of the new. Into that gap the visionaries and creatives, the pioneers of the new journey, move and begin to experiment. They also talk to each other, network, form alliances and collaborations. In such a way these small and scattered experiments, in the liminal space between the old and new, begin to scale up and form the kind of sustainable and resilient structures of a new system.[1]

Wheatley and Frieze also describe some of the main agents within this theory of change. Firstly there are the pioneers, or 'walk outs' as they call them, who have the courage and the vision to 'walk out' of one system in order to forge the new. These are the entrepreneurs and the innovators, the inventors and creatives whose love for the old system and all it provided compels them into a journey of reimagination. Such people need space from the assumptions and scepticism of the old system.

Organizations and institutions are predisposed to maintain the stability of the status quo. That is what they are designed to do: to create a stable and reliable environment for the provision or delivery of what the system is there for. Most of the time that works fine. But when the environment around the system changes significantly, new answers to the same questions need to be found, and initially at least these will be challenged by the innate disposition of the system to preserve itself. So, as the Catholic anthropologist and writer Gerald Arbuckle says, 'the new belongs elsewhere'. In order for new answers to old questions to be found in a new context, space must be given to those with the gift of finding them. Arbuckle puts it like this: 'A refounding project should not normally be placed in the midst of existing work/structures, where prophetic people would be under constant critical assessment by members of the community and required to waste valuable energy "apologizing" for that they are doing.'[2]

Then there are those who champion the innovators. These agents of change are not pioneers themselves but champion the pioneers from within the old system, rooting for them, encouraging them and making space for them. They do this by defending them, by affirming them, by naming their work as legitimate, by helping articulate the story of this new work in ways that makes connections with the old.

There are also those who act to 'hospice' the old system, who recognize that there is an important work in allowing the old to die well, honouring its contribution and giving it the space, time and attention that recognizes that the life it has had is coming to an end. 'Hospicers' do that incredibly important work of attending to the remnants of the old system, caring for those still living within that old dispensation. But they do so with no illusion that the old system is suddenly going to spark into life again. They do not give any kind of false promises about a return to the halcyon days when the old system was full of life and at the heart of things. 'Hospicers' have little time for the fantasies of nostalgia. They carry out the gentle and compassionate work of allowing something the dignity of a good death, of helping a group or a community, or even a whole organization, to let go and face the reality of the end of its life.

☩

Death is something the church could and should be talking about in a prophetic way within a society (particularly a British one) that struggles to do so. The church really should be able to do death! After all, Christianity does death. The symbol of

Christianity is a device for killing people. We are brazen in our assertion of death at the heart of our faith, a particular death that leads to a universal offer of life. The trajectory of our faith is life through death, death as a necessary element in the liberation into new life.

Yet we aren't very good at talking about death in the public sphere. This may well be because we are all too aware of the fact that it's not a subject that the public particularly want to engage with. It's much easier to join with discussions on how to care for and keep people alive than suggest an honest conversation about the reality of death and finitude. Maybe we're not so comfortable with death ourselves.

Sam Wells argues that there was a point when something changed in the way we talk about the fundamentals of the Christian faith. He argues that in the mid-nineteenth century people began to stop believing in hell. And as a result the message of the gospel has shifted away from a focus on the issue of our ultimate fate beyond death to the issue of the fullness (or otherwise) of our life now.[3] No doubt this is a good thing in many ways. It has done away with the dubious practice of preaching warnings of hell rather than the invitation to life in Christ. It also brings back into play the majority of the gospel story between the credal statements 'born of the virgin Mary' and 'suffered under Pontius Pilate'. But has this shift also dimmed our confidence in speaking about matters of eternity, matters of not just life but also death?

Death does seem an almost taboo subject when it comes to talking about churches. We embrace the idea of church growth, church planting, church multiplication – all organic metaphors for church life – and yet rarely do we talk about church death. Yet we should be keenly aware of church death from our history. You only have to read the New Testament, perhaps most forcefully the Book of Revelation, to realize that many church communities are not for ever. Nevertheless we act as though the churches of our own experience are a given, with a right to eternally exist, and that it is our role to protect them.

Of course, no one wants to see a church close. And there is

every reason to lament and grieve such an event when it happens. No doubt, sometimes churches do close when there is still life and witness in them, a premature death if you like. But in the same way there are churches that are essentially in palliative care for which the most dignified thing we can do is gently and gracefully allow them to die.

I have a small plot in my garden where I do my best to grow a few veg every year. One of the joys at the beginning of each season is to open up the compost heap, which through the winter has been slowly transforming the surplus organic matter from the end of last season into the black, odourless and rich resource to kick-start the next. Nothing is wasted in nature. Everything is recycled. Every death has the promise of life hidden within it. New life emerges from deaths transformed. Nature is a circular ecology. So what might it mean to talk about a circular ecology of church? Where we might embrace a cycle of life and death, where death is not just the end of life but critical to its beginning?

There is a tree that grows in the tropical regions between Costa Rica and Columbia which is commonly known as the suicide tree. These slow-growing trees reach heights of 100 feet with large, buttressed trunks. Suicide trees produce fruit and seeds only once in their lifetime and, perhaps most remarkably, once they have done this the tree slowly dies and falls to the forest floor. Why? A number of reasons have been suggested. But one reason is that in its dying the parent tree provides two things essential to the flourishing of its offspring – light and nutrients. A circular ecology.

This is not a binary argument for the closure of 'old' established churches up and down the country to make space for the new and innovative. But perhaps we might be willing to move towards a more theological view of church death. It is absolutely natural and right that, like Dylan Thomas, we 'rage against the dying of the light'. That means lamenting the decline and senescence of death which is painful and which feels unjust. But equally we have to be open to being midwives to a good death of churches in many places. Deaths that we will want to grieve and lament, but in which we must look for the seeds of the future.

☩

For David and Jo, it's clearly been a challenge holding space for the new while being faithful to the old. The old is represented by the 13 churches in the town of Beaminster and its surrounding villages. These villages read like the lines of a Betjeman poem; Toller Pocorum, Drimpton, Solway Ash, Melplash, Mosterton. Navigating that challenge has involved trusting in the theology of vocation and the abundance of God. They invited anyone to join in with the new developments that Jo was starting by encouraging people to explore the new as part of their vocation. They trusted that, as people began to help with new things like toddler groups and Messy Church, God would provide. God has provided. At the same time there has also been a reduction in the sheer volume of traditional services. There has been a rebalancing. There has been some dying.

I drive to Drimpton through the deep summer lanes of this remote part of Dorset. Amazingly, a village of only 400 people continues to support a pub, a village hall, a recreation ground, a Methodist chapel and the small church of St Mary's. However, the deeper changes impacting rural villages like this are at work here too. David tells me that the pub is under threat of closure and the cricket club struggles to keep going. Meanwhile the church is starting to admit that it is coming to the end of its present journey. 'Five years ago', says David, 'we had the Bishop here to celebrate the 150th anniversary of the new building being consecrated, and five years on, it's gone downhill to the point where there are lots of people worshipping, regularly 12, 13, 14, 15 people. But nobody will take on any roles.' We laugh that a congregation of maximum 15 people is considered 'lots of people worshipping' but when that works out as nearly 4% of the population of the village it compares favourably with proportions of people attending church nationally. The challenge once more is the age and energy needed to resource the requirements of the upkeep and maintenance of the building. 'Two men, one churchwarden, one licensed lay minister, who have kept it going said, "We can't do this on our own anymore." I mean, they're getting older and older.'

The church of St Mary's is a building not dissimilar in design to All Saints in Stour Row, though significantly smaller. A small wooden porch has been added on to the front door, lending an air of progress and development. I have brought some lunch and sit on a sun-bleached wooden bench in the shade behind the church. The long narrow graveyard stretches away from me, the older graves nearest the church submerged by the summer grass. Strips of access have been cut in this meadow for walking to the newer graves at the back. Beyond these, through a gap in some hawthorn trees, lies another open space, empty, waiting in the summer heat.

These consecrated fields demonstrate both the challenge and the potential of the gulf between the inherited traditions of the church and the life of the villages in which they are held. At another parish in the Beaminster team David describes how the worshipping community have shifted their posture towards the village community, changing the nature of their worship but also taking the bold decision to begin to make use of their land in new ways. Not long before David arrived an extension to the graveyard was consecrated with room for 300 graves. David has since buried six people there in 13 years. It's unlikely that all that space for graves is needed. So the community have taken a risk against the grain of traditional assumptions and planted a community apple orchard. The hope is that the apples can be a free resource for the whole community and the orchard a venue for cider pressing days.

These decisions play out the contested nature of these and other spaces associated with the inherited church. For some what is at stake is the preservation of the church and its function as the traditional provider of services of worship and rites of passage. But in other places these harder red lines around monuments of ecclesial heritage are being blurred. Communities of faith are experimenting with the posture of tradition in these places, exploring how the gulf can be bridged from both sides and whether a new kind of faith community might well be able to meet in the middle, one that has been formed through a conversation developed together.

David and Jo describe the conversation between the traditional and the new life that is emerging. What they describe feels like two people divided by language and culture, with David, Jo and others acting as translators and arbitrators between them. The cultural gulf is great. Jo wonders if it's possible to bridge it at all. 'I feel the gulf between [the new] and what happens on a Sunday seems to get wider and wider in lots of ways. In 30 years' time, will my toddler mums be running the church? I don't think they will.' Jo reflects whether more work might have been done to bridge the gap from both ends. She cites recent academic research into rural ministry and the fragility of so many rural churches that concludes that intentional discipleship is the only viable response to the uncertain future of these many churches.[4] It leaves Jo reflecting whether things might have turned out differently if innovation had gone hand in hand with discipleship of the existing church communities. 'I just think if we had done this experiment differently, and if we had just focused on discipling the current congregations when I got here, before we started doing anything new, would we have had a different outcome? And the answer is, I don't know.'

Either way it's clear there is no quick fix, no magic formula to the dilemmas and challenges of the church looking to find a renewal of life in the context of a secular age. Planting an orchard at the edge of a graveyard seems like an apt metaphor for the sort of attitude that the church might take. A kind of investment of faith in a shared future that is a conversation between the living tradition of faith and the communities around it. A long-term project of vulnerable, shared construction that

ST MARY'S, DRIMPTON, DORSET

doesn't retreat from the reality and very possibility of death for much of what has been held so precious for so many for so long. You cannot rush discipleship. And from both sides of the gulf it's clear that discipleship is the heart of the matter, journeying with those engaging with the church in new ways toward a maturity of faith, and journeying with those who have held these traditions for their whole lives to enable them to embrace the potential for the Spirit's reimagining. That this is a death, a loss, is true. Death and loss are within the trajectory of the gospel. Time is not only linear but circular. The Kingdom is a paradoxical economy, a circular economy. So the inevitable march of decline may yet herald a resurrection beyond death, held in the seeds of an apple in a newly planted garden.

Out of the relationships generated by Jo's ministry a small new community of faith has begun to emerge. It's a fragile expression of new life finding its place somewhere in the liminal space between the communities of the Beaminster villages and the inherited life of the church. The emergence of this community has been slow and unsteady. Attempts to invite parents from Messy Church into a journey of discipleship themselves led one Lent to a gathering in Jo's house. The group drank gin and tonic and talked about faith. But then Covid hit and other things took priority until Jo revived the group online over a year later. She emailed invitations to all her contacts and five people turned up, which morphed into ten people meeting regularly online to drink gin, discuss the Bible together and pray for each other.

Like the toys hidden behind the pulpit and the altar, Gin Church, as it has become known, feels like a hidden expression of new life, unseen and unheralded by the ongoing tradition. Until out of the blue Jenny, one of the regular members of Gin Church who has been coming for two years, starts to inquire about getting baptized.[5] Not long after that it's Easter and Jenny asks which Easter service would be the best for her to come to.

A quick reflection and Jo suggests that she come to the sunrise service at one of the churches in the benefice. It's a service full of traditional liturgy and symbolism. As the sun rises and spring light seeps into the air a fire is lit. Then the new Paschal candle is lit and brought into church to symbolize the new life of Jesus risen from the dead. And there is water and drama as people are sprinkled with water from the font to remind them of the new life at work in them. This would surely be a good service for a new disciple to attend.

And there is a moment when Jo wonders if she should ring Jenny up and say that this might be a good moment for her to follow through with her interest in getting baptized. But in the end she thinks better of it. Just coming to a church on Easter Sunday at 6am might be enough without making her the centre of attention. But Jo also knows that part of the tradition at the sunrise service has been to ask if there is anyone there that wants to renew their baptism vows. Is David going to be doing that again this year? Yes, he is. But Jo decides not to make any explicit invitation and instead trust the Spirit and see what happens.

Standing next to her, Jo guides Jenny through the service until the moment comes when David asks the congregation if anyone would like to be renew their baptism vows or be baptized for the first time. Jenny looks at Jo with a meaningful look of inquiry. Jo shrugs her shoulders and raises her eyebrows as if to say, 'Why not?!' And so Jenny comes forward out of the gloom of the chancel as the sun rises outside on Easter morning in a little village in rural east Dorset and is baptized. And the small congregation of the faithful from across the 13 villages of the benefice laugh and cry and rejoice as a liturgy that rehearses and retells a timeless truth becomes present reality before their eyes. New life has come. Someone invisible to them has come from death to life in their midst. The living tradition held by that old building has just welcomed a new disciple from the community in which it has stood for centuries. The timeless story of the gospel, which insists that the constant surprise of new life in the Spirit must follow the experience of alienation and death, has been told again. And the gulf between the secular age and the old inheritances of tradition has been bridged, as a liturgy that might so easily decline into formula becomes fully alive in the person of Jenny.

Notes

1 Wheatley and Frieze, *Walk Out Walk On*.
2 Arbuckle, *Refounding the Church*, pp. 119, 151.
3 Wells, *A Future That's Bigger than the Past*, pp. 6–9.
4 Francis, 'Taking discipleship learning seriously; setting priorities for the rural church'.
5 Jenny is not her real name.

PART 2

Waiting

'The future must enter you
a long time before it happens.'

Rainer Rilke

The Manual and the Measure – A Parable

The Kingdom of God is like an estate owner who went on a long journey to a distant land. Before he left he gathered his tenants and gave them responsibility for all the work of the estate until his return.

He gave them freedom to expand the estate into new areas and to build new barns for the harvest. The tenants asked. 'How will we know where to plant crops and what kind of barns to build?' 'Remember me, and everything I've taught you, listen to the land and to the wind in the trees,' said the estate owner. 'And you will know what to do.'

So the tenants set to work, planting new crops in new places and preparing for the harvest. When the harvest came they began to build a new barn and when it was finished the harvest was gathered into it. The next year they planted new crops in new places again and built new barns. It was hard work but the rewards were great. People were getting busier and busier and did little else but plant crops and build new barns. And the years came and went and the estate expanded, with new crops and new barns.

The people from other estates came and asked how they could repeat their success. The tenants got together and produced a manual and a measure. A manual on how to farm and a measure to ensure that every new barn built was like the first.

Then one year the estate's expansion brought the tenants to a new area. An area unlike the valley of the estate. An area of hills and dry soil. They planted their crops and they built the barns according to the manual and the measure. But the crops failed and the barn nearly collapsed in the strong winds on the hillside. That same year reports began to come in from the other estates. People had used the manual and the measure. In some cases it had worked really well. But in others crops had struggled and the barns were a costly expense for such a small harvest.

The tenants met and asked, 'What shall we do?' An argument developed between them. Some said that the manual and the measure had always worked – 'Work harder, and all will be well!' But others pointed to the hillsides where the crops had failed and where the barns were empty and dilapidated. They said how tired people were of working without reward. They reminded the tenants of the estate owner's parting words – 'Remember me … and you will know what to do.'

Just then the estate owner returned. He saw the fields of crops stretching into the distance and the barns raised high above the fields. And yet he was sad. 'Master!' said the tenants. 'Come and see our fields of crops and the great many barns we have built!' 'I have seen your barns and your fields of wheat,' said the estate owner, 'but as I travelled here have I not also seen people working hard and spending money they do not have on planting crops that will not grow and repairing barns that will never be full?'

And the estate owner stayed talking with the tenants into the depths of the night. The tenants begged the estate owner to stay so that they could convince him that their manual and measure would work in time. The estate owner listened graciously and said nothing until he retired to sleep. 'Remember me, and everything I've taught you, listen to the land and to the wind in the trees,' he said. 'And you will know what to do.' And in the morning he had gone.

4

Oak Tree Anglican Fellowship, Acton, London

After leaving university I took myself off to Kenya to teach in a church-sponsored school. Famously, Africans say, 'You westerners have all the watches but we Africans have the time.' In the remote and arid part of Kenya where I had been based, the journey back to Nairobi involved waiting for a 'matatu' (a public bus) at the end of our road. There was no timetable for this bus. It left in the morning and came back in the afternoon.

In practice there was a good chance you could wait for an hour before a cloud of dust and a smudge of diesel fumes on the horizon heralded its arrival. This reality was something you gradually learnt to embrace and even enjoy. Waiting with nothing to do but wait became enjoyable. You could not use the time for anything else. This was a full kind of waiting, attentive to the possibility of the bus's arrival at any moment, yet free enough to enable the kind of conversation and engagement with others that you often don't have at other times. When I arrived back from Kenya I was living in London just as real-time displays had been introduced on London's bus routes. How useful! A display that told you how many minutes of your precious time you were going to have to waste waiting for your bus! Now in theory this was designed to take the wait out of waiting. In theory this innovation removed the anxiety associated with the lack of control experienced in the process of waiting. But in reality it meant that everyone stared at a digital display, willing the number of minutes for the bus to go steadily down, anxiety rising as the reading resolutely failed to change despite the passing of time.

Immediately after that year in Kenya, I volunteered to work as a youth and children's worker with a parish church in the east end of Glasgow. I lived for a year looking out on Barlinnie Prison from the second floor of a tenement block in Ruchazie, Greater Easterhouse. Ruchazie had a reputation far worse than the reality. Nevertheless, the reality for someone who had grown up in the quiet tranquillity of Stour Row, where drama involved nothing more exciting than some cattle loose on the road, was that Ruchazie was the wild west. Two weeks after I arrived I returned to my flat one Sunday afternoon to find the door kicked down and the flat ransacked. With a kind of sympathetic but resigned compassion towards the inevitability of these events, the church community relocated the Sunday evening service to my flat while my front door was rehung. This was something of a rite of passage.

Over that year I experienced the enduring love and faith of a struggling Christian community. They were custodians of a building that looked more like a fortress than a church, covered as it was in barbed wire and security features. They were a church deeply engaged in its community through youth work, children's work and a vibrant credit union. Yet the building looked as though we were at constant war with an invading malevolence harbouring in the community. They were an ageing church with plenty of folk who could still tell you the story of Ruchazie from its creation. They could tell you of the excitement and the hope of being offered flats in these gleaming new tenements on the edge of the city, up and out from the slums, high up where the air was clearer overlooking the clutter of the city. Where new flats had inside toilets instead of a privy and more space than you could dream of. This was a church living in the reality that that dream, that vision of town planners and architects, had failed. And of all the theories of why it failed, perhaps the most convincing is that what poor communities have, perhaps more than any other communities, is a depth of social capital and a resilience of community that helps transcend and mitigate against the realities of inequality. But ripping communities up from the roots of their story and from the interconnectedness of their shared life takes much of that resilience from them. Place and community are emergent gifts, formed slowly through generations of lived experience. You cannot plan place over a matter of a few years. You cannot manufacture community. The outer estates of Glasgow and other major cities imagined that new utopian neighbourhoods on the green fringes of the city would somehow enable these communities to make a new and brighter start. But what they failed to do was account for the critical importance of deep social ties and relational capital in the ongoing formation of good community.

Back in London, I took this deep experience of the alienation of community from itself and managed to enrol myself on a

Master's course in urban policy. My wife and I had joined a church in Acton, west London. So we found ourselves pitching up on Sunday afternoons with a group of people who had planted this church some two or three years earlier. We had attached ourselves to the beginnings of what would become one of the most significant church planting movements in the Anglican church, the Holy Trinity Brompton network of churches. With my degree in urban policy, within two years of joining the church I found myself leading on the church's engagement with the wider community of Acton. Acton was in receipt of significant amounts of money from the Government's Single Regeneration Budget. Our vicar had been invited to be on the board of the organization delivering the programme funded by this money. He wanted to ensure that the churches in Acton had a practical involvement in the programme of social regeneration that was taking place. So I was asked to lead a project that acted as something of an interface between the churches in Acton and regeneration of the wider community.

It was an impossible job. I thought there would be a natural inclination for the church to engage alongside others in the regeneration of its community. I produced a handbook of volunteering opportunities that made it easy for people to connect their skills and interests with the sort of openings for service and engagement that there were in the community. Of course, there were individuals who got it and stories of connection, service and sacrifice that made it all worthwhile. But by and large the church looked on from a distance, thought the project good and noble, said it would pray for it, and carried on with its own business.

What I grappled with in that job was something I am only beginning to understand now. My uphill struggle to engage the church in the long slow work of relationship building and in the love of a community and place was not the struggle to get agreement. It was not a struggle to win a theological argument for the work I was doing. It was not a struggle to get support from the church that this was a worthwhile thing to be doing. It was a struggle against how people unthinkingly oriented their lives. It was a struggle against the cultural assumptions that people live by. It was against the prevailing version of what Charles Taylor calls a 'social imaginary'. Taylor describes a social imaginary as 'The way in which [people] imagine their social existence, how they fit together with others, how things go on between them and their fellows, the expectations which are normally met, and the deeper normative notions and images which underlie these expectations.'[1] I was discovering that the social imaginary of the church community did not have a great deal of space, or time, for the complex and fragmented world that lay in the immediate place beyond their door.

It became clear that for most people the place in which they lived had very little call on their time or attention. People led incredibly busy and engaged lives. We were a church of predominantly young professionals, getting married, having children, and finding our way around this huge city for work, leisure, entertainment and so on. Few of us had lived in Acton for any length of time. We were all incomers. It was unlikely to be somewhere we would live for the rest of our lives. It certainly wasn't somewhere we had grown up in. It was a space in which we lived. But it wasn't our place.[2]

I wanted to love Acton. We felt called to be there and had taken the risk of buying a flat there rather than living somewhere cheaper, so that we could live in the community in which the church met. I naively expected that other people wanted to love Acton too and would want to express that love for place by coming alongside people, people not like us, in order to build relationship and help shape community. And of course there were those who did. But they were a minority. Like Sarah, who started a Community Association in her street and motivated people to attend to some of the issues that were taking place there. Or a lady called Fatima, who had started a skills cooperative in a vacant shop on the large social housing estate in the centre of Acton, to which growing numbers of residents, many of them refugees, began to come to learn how to sew or use a computer, and to use those skills to gain employment or start small businesses. However, these expressions of community were oases of connection amidst a desert of ephemeral relationships and disconnection from place.

Where was I finding community? On reflection it was with people who had time. Those who had found ways of giving up paid work in order to give time to their local community. Or who had simply opted out of the fast-paced life of London employment and found a different kind of life on their doorstep. Those who had come to the country with nothing but who had the time to forge new relationships and communities of connection in the vacant spaces of the city. Those in disadvantaged communities, high-rise blocks, under-resourced estates whose place had chosen them, but who had chosen to fight for the richness of community as a kind of resistance to the sense of abandonment.

☦

What I have come to discover is that time is the issue, and time is the problem. Not time itself. But the way in which we have come to regard time in our modern world. Time is accelerating. Modern life is accelerating and drawing us into the logic of its own acceleration. This is a practical reality. Researchers measured the speed at which people walk in different cities around the globe. There is a direct correlation between modern urban development and the speed at which people walk. People who move from rural areas into cities start to walk faster. Not only that but when researchers return to cities and measure the speed that people walk ten years later, they discover that people's pace of walking has speeded up again.[3] This is the practical expression of the logic of acceleration in modern life. In the US an investment firm recognized that it could garner an advantage if it could improve the speed of transactions between Chicago and New York. By building a new cable between the two cities and cutting the time of connection down by just a fraction of a second it could attract business to its platform and build a significant share of the market. Instead of using existing railway lines as a route for the new cable, Spread Networks built a new cable in a direct line between Chicago and New York, forcing their way through any obstacle to achieve their aim. The result was a four-millisecond improvement in the time in which transactions could be communicated. But that was enough to ensure that anyone wanting to gain an advantage in the lucrative derivative markets came to them.[4]

At university I was teased for how slowly I was capable of walking around the place, a legacy surely of years in living in Stour Row, walking the dog down the lane on days with little else to do. Having all the time in the world. In London I just couldn't do that anymore. I walked with purpose and speed, anxious to get where I was going in as little time as possible. I was now like everyone else, trying to cut corners, beat the queue, play the system as efficiently as possible. And I didn't know how to do it in any other way. I had not chosen to speed up my approach to life. It just happened by stealth, the speed of the world around me moulding me to its pace and drive.

So it was no coincidence that most people had little time to engage with their local community despite thinking this a noble aim. It was also no coincidence that those who did invest in the community around them were those who had time. Because it's time that is at the root of our dislocated relationship with place. John Swinton explains how time has developed in our modern world into a commodity, a resource, not something that is gifted but something that must be grasped and utilized in service to human endeavour. In pre-modern times there were really only three times in the day – sunrise, high noon and sunset. Time was oriented through the experience of creation in ways that couldn't be controlled. It was the Benedictines who first invented ways in which time could be measured. The first clocks were used by the monastics to divide up the day into hours. Before then they divided up the day into hours using an hourglass. In some monasteries a monk was given the task of staying up all night looking after the hourglass until it was time to call the monks together for the first time of prayer of the day.

The new mechanical clocks were a more efficient way of doing the same thing. A way of regulating the routines of the monastery. But as Swinton makes clear, this was not about owning time, rather it was about regularizing the monks' ability to participate in *God's time*. He says: 'The development of these early mechanical clocks emerged in an attempt to bind monks into the timefulness of God. Spiritual time was not scheduled into the day. Each aspect of every day was conceived as irresistibly and irrefutably spiritual. Each event was participating in a timeful whole within which the clock was a reminder and a call toward a higher power.'[5]

Having been invented, the clock escaped from the monastery. It soon became clear that an invention designed to help attend to the timefulness of God could be used to manage the affairs of human beings. Clocks became the centre pieces of cities, alongside, but ultimately in competition with, the bells of churches which by then were the successors of those early monastic devices calling the people to prayer. The development of clocks goes hand in hand with the development of commerce, trade and industry. It becomes an indispensable tool in the ability of humanity to make production and trade regular and efficient. Through the advances of modernism, time was fundamentally severed from its spiritual origins. Time was 'put to work shaping, sustaining, and guiding the new economics. Gone were its spiritual roots and values.'[6] As a result 'we have become people who think we have to fit God in rather than fit in with what God is doing'.[7]

If time then is a commodity to be used, a resource among others to spend in order to serve our own ambitions and service our own projects, it becomes perfectly consistent to make as much use of that time as possible. Every hour, every minute, every second must be used to the greatest extent possible. Time is a currency to be invested to create as much return as possible. Critically, time is no longer a gift of God but a resource for producing or getting more. It has become a means of having, not a part of simply being or of participating in the presence of the Giver of Time. There becomes only one kind of activity regarded as legitimate in the modern world, the kind of activity that is about producing, about getting, about having.

At 'Oak Tree', as our church was called, I remember someone who worked for a large bank in the city. Graham and his family were like the rest of us at Oak Tree, finding our way in the professional life of London at the time, making a living to enable us to get a mortgage, live somewhere and raise a family. For a season my wife and I were in the same weekly housegroup with Graham. Though we rarely saw him. On the rare occasions he made it to the group he was ragged and tired and not really able to contribute to the content of the evening. On one occasion he told us there was a joke going round the office. When you met someone in a lift and asked, 'How are you?' people would raise a wry smile and reply: "I haven't had time to check.'

Activity that is purely about having breeds more busyness, which legitimates itself as good activity because that's the only activity there is. But the consequences are not good. The more I try and keep up with the internal logic of this kind of activity, the more busy I become and the more disconnected from myself and the world around me. I experience a kind of alienation which encompasses both self and place. This is a point made by Andrew Root, drawing on the work of German philosopher Hartmut Rosa. Rosa's argument is that the busyness and consequent 'time-famine' of the modern world means we become disconnected from our experience of life. Andrew Root summarizes Rosa's thinking like this: 'We're cut off from the reality that there is more than our individual identity projects and the race to harvest resources for some undefined dream.'[8] This alienation is experienced because 'the more energy I expend, becoming busier in my activity, the more I'm alienated from the givenness of the world. Soon the exhaustion of this expenditure of energy, to have as much of the givenness of reality as I want, alienates me from myself. And, worse, being alienated from myself, I'm alienated from the world.'[9]

Being at Oak Tree in those formative years was intoxicating because we were a growing church. The long shadow of decline was already beginning to cast its gloom over the church. We had come to the end of the decade of evangelism and it was clear that the hope that this strategy might reverse decline had been misplaced. London Diocese, however, was bucking the trend, and to some extent this was the result of the beginnings of a church planting movement of which Oak Tree was most definitely a part. A great deal of research and prayer had been undertaken before it was agreed that Oak Tree would begin. That research had identified Acton as a place where the existing parishes of the area were not succeeding in mission to their communities. They were in decline. They were not growing. What was needed was a new approach built on the success of other church plants in London that had successfully revitalized struggling churches in other areas.

Oak Tree therefore adopted what has now become a well-worn formula of planting from one thriving church into an area where the church is struggling, often taking on a redundant building or one where the congregation has shrunk to unsustainable numbers. In our case we started life in one of the existing parish buildings, meeting in the afternoon, before moving into a local school. We had staff from the word go and from our inception the resources to lay on a service of worship, much like other churches in the HTB family. And we did grow. Mainly we grew from people moving to the area, like us, and joining the church. But we also grew with a small but steady influx of people who were becoming Christians through courses like Alpha.

I was at Oak Tree for a few years before I felt a call to ordination and moved away to train to be a vicar. I am always hugely grateful for those years there. Oak Tree was a good church, a loving community, with a group of people who genuinely sought to live out their faith in the daily lives and in the context of their community. We were explicit in our commitment to the place of Acton, referring to ourselves as a 'Church *for* Acton'. And yet somehow we struggled to really 'be' a church for that place. In spending time with some of the other vicars of the parish churches in the area, churches that were struggling by and large, certainly not growing to the extent we were, I sensed that inherent connection with place that was fostered by being a church with history and long-term connection with that fragment of London given to their concern and care. Could Oak Tree ever be that kind of church? Would we have to be a parish church in the classic sense with all the responsibilities and (at times) burdens that that would place upon us? Perhaps it was in that little word 'for' that our struggles to relate to Acton lay. We were invariably church for Acton on our own terms. We struggled to relate to the community around us except by seeing it as a potential resource for the activities that we delivered; services, mission events, Alpha courses etc. Seeing the community as a place to be with people, for their sakes and on their terms, or at least on equal terms, did not fit so easily with how we saw things.

Though of course the thing is that that was not how we 'saw things', consciously at least. In the same way that Charles Taylor speaks of a 'social imaginary' I think we might also speak of an 'ecclesial imaginary'. An 'ecclesial imaginary' describes how we internalize our way of being church in the world. And it's not something we tend to question. That's the point of 'imaginaries', they are the internal framework of understanding that we carry with us in the world. They make life possible in a very efficient way, saving us the bother of constantly having to work things out from first principles.

The ecclesial imaginary that we have developed in the modern world is one that asserts the church as the main agent of mission in the world. Taylor argues that the move into the modern era was driven to some extent by a process of 'disenchantment'. In this process all that is mysterious and beyond our understanding need not be given over to concepts like spirits or gods but can be explained in material terms. And while the church resisted this, it has become implicated in a view of the world that makes a much greater emphasis on human action. Without a sense of the world as God's gift, or without the sense that there is some greater cosmic significance to the world around us, human beings begin to see the world as something to be ordered and exploited for their own benefit. While God may yet be present in his design or order, the cosmos has essentially been disenchanted and the previously reliable status quo disrupted. The void that is left behind must be filled by our own effort, our own organization and our own industry in the world.[10]

The concern with this imaginary, however, is the place it makes for the church. It makes the church the main agent of mission. The star of the show. However, I am not convinced the church was ever meant to be the star of the show. Jesus' message gave priority to the Kingdom of God. The gospels mention the Kingdom of God hundreds of times, while the word 'ecclesia', which translates as 'church', is mentioned twice. Furthermore, as I read Acts in particular, the picture I get is not one of the church setting the agenda, organizing itself for mission, setting out some sort of strategy and putting it into action. It is not a picture of a church mobilizing itself into the world, asserting a sense of its own identity on the world. Instead, the image from the book of Acts is one of a community of disciples desperately discerning how to align its action with the movement of the Spirit which is moving ahead of it. The church forms in the wake of this missionary Spirit. The church is the result of the movement of the Spirit, of a bunch a disciples walking 'haphazardly into the Kingdom of God'[11] through the leading of the Spirit which forms this new people of God in its wake. So the church, called and inaugurated by Jesus, is the creation of the Spirit. Which means that the church is not the star of the show, God is, through the presence of Jesus and the power of the Spirit. The church is made more peripheral, less central, more ec-centric by the central role played by the Spirit in the ongoing work of God's mission. Steve Bevans puts it like this:

> Being a church created by the Spirit is always to be a church 'on the edge', a little unsure of itself (not of its Lord!), always in discernment. This is because ... the Spirit goes ahead of the church, challenging it as it follows the Spirit in its mission,

indeed leading into the new beyond its often scarred imagination, beyond what it had conceived as unchangeable and divinely-given laws.[12]

The ironic thing is that in many ways we were a church 'on the edge', on the edge of the complex community of Acton. And yet we spoke and often acted out a vision, certainly a dream, that we would inhabit its centre. We were part of a movement that was apparently reversing the decline being experienced by the church elsewhere, a movement that was renewing declined or vacant churches and experiencing rapid growth. Growth and a return to the kind of impact and influence that churches had enjoyed in generations past seemed part of the sub-text of what was taking place. Was this renewal? Or re-newal? A turning back of the clock to a time of church strength, church significance and church influence. Churches transforming society, pushing back the tide of secularism. These narratives were tempting to my young mind at the time, as we left London and headed west to embark on two years of training for my ordination into the Church of England. I had every intention of playing my part in the unfolding story of church renewal. However, it was a story that would get considerably more complex and unpredictable than the neat narrative I travelled with as Acton grew smaller in the rear-view mirror.

Notes

1 Taylor, *A Secular Age*, pp. 171–2.
2 For an excellent discussion about the difference between space and place see Foulger, *Present in Every Place?*, Ch. 1.
3 Colville, *The Great Acceleration, how the world is getting faster and faster*, pp. 1–3.
4 Colville, pp. 235–6.
5 Swinton, *Becoming Friends of Time*, p. 28.
6 Swinton, p. 29.
7 Swinton, p. 30.
8 Root, *The Congregation in a Secular Age*, p. 167.
9 Root, *Churches and the Crisis of Decline*, p. 129. 'Givenness'

here means the knowable reality of the world. The modern world, Root argues, has bracketed out any concept of the transcendent and assumes that all reality is given. There is nothing that is 'non-given'. This is essentially a materialist position that argues that what we see and experience, what we can measure and know with our rational aptitude, is the sum total of all there is.

10 Taylor, *A Secular Age*, pp. 423–72.

11 A phrase from U. A. Fanthorpe's wonderful poem 'BC:AD', Fanthorpe, *Selected Poems*.

12 Bevans, 'The Church as the creation of the Spirit', p. 15.

5

St Alban's, Norwich

Toward the end of my time training for ordination, something fairly extraordinary happened in the life of the Church of England. In 2004 it produced a report that became something of a bestseller. Thousands of copies of *Mission-Shaped Church* were sold, read and reflected on across not just the Church of England but other denominations as well.[1] The report spawned a movement, Fresh Expressions, which developed from its Anglican beginnings into a multi-denominational and international movement of networks exploring, promoting and enabling new expressions of church in a whole variety of settings.[2]

Mission-Shaped Church offered a deep reflection on the cultural context for mission at the beginning of the twenty-first century. It accurately described the realities of the missional context facing the church. It recognized that if the church was to engage with society along the grain of the culture of modern Britain, rather than against it, it would have to do more than simply set up shop in a community and invite people to come. *Mission-Shaped Church* advocated a missional theology that saw the Holy Spirit as the vanguard of mission. And it saw the role of the church as a participant in that mission, venturing out from the safety and comfort of its own stilted imagination and starting to allow the Holy Spirit, and the context in which the Spirit was already present, to shape new expressions of church.

As *Mission-Shaped Church* landed in the studies of church leaders across the country, I was cutting my teeth as a curate in a large parish in Southampton with two church buildings. My generous training vicar gave me space to explore some of the principles from *Mission-Shaped Church* which were already part of my DNA, but which had been given a kind of viral boost by the affirmation of what I was reading in that report. The cultural gap between our services on Sunday and the community in which I walked my kids to school was clearly huge. I had my eye on a disused unit in the local shopping area down the hill, a million cultural miles from the church up the road. I hounded the landlords and persuaded them to offer me the shop for a month for next to nothing. A team formed and we transformed this quirky area into an exhibition space for the week of Easter, in which we told the story of the prodigal son using various artistic media, video, installation and imagery. It was a rich and crazy time, working to pull something together for which I had only a fraction of the necessary skills and gifts. But 500 people came through that exhibition and hung out in the café we created as an expression of the radical grace and hospitality of the community party at the end of the story. Many of those people wrote profound things in the visitors' book about how the exhibition had affected them.

These experiments in imaginative retellings of the gospel story acted as a kind of kindergarten for my own development as a missional leader among those with few if any of the common cultural assumptions of a Christian heritage. As I came to the end of my four years as a curate I took the decision that this was where I felt called to keep exploring. While there were few opportunities around at that time that would make this possible, I persevered, and just as time was beginning to run out on the house in which we lived, I secured a role as a pioneer minister in Poole, Dorset. After 18 years away from the county of my upbringing I had found my way back to Dorset. I was coming home.

This itself proved to be quite formative. I was starting to engage with the story of St Francis and as I did I began to make connections with his own homecoming. The story of the beginning of the Franciscan movement commonly hinges around a moment of Francis' life in the church of St Damian in Assisi. Having returned to his hometown from military endeavours, bewildered and humiliated by sickness, Francis took to praying in front of the crucifix in the church. One day as he carried out this practice, he heard a voice say, 'Francis, seest thou not that my house is in ruins? Go and restore it for me.'[3] Upon this experience the course and story of his life changed. Francis immediately set about gathering materials and resources to embark on the project of physically restoring the church in Assisi. But it then became clear to Francis that this very strategic and logical response to the vision was not what God was asking of him. On the contrary, God's invitation required a total surrender of Francis' abilities to gather resources, plan and assert his leadership on the existing institution of the church. Francis began again, this time with a tiny group of fellow disciples in the exposed crypt of the church, praying for spiritual renewal and offering their lives in service to the poor.

As I read these stories of the life of Francis I began to pray and reflect on the connections that might be made in terms of renewal of the church in our own time. The church planting movement that I had left behind in London was gathering momentum, beginning to spill out of its birth cradle in the capital and into other parts of the country. Churches were being revitalized. Old buildings on the cusp of closure were being filled with people, making new disciples, offering programmes and projects to the poor and marginalized in their communities. Somehow I felt called to something different. I don't think God was condemning the initial efforts of Francis to restore the church in the way that seemed most immediately obvious. Instead, God was calling Francis to something far beyond the time, scale and limited scope of his own imaginings, standing as he must have done looking at the dilapidated state of one church building in the hills of Assisi. It was a call to follow the Spirit into the future and to leave his blueprint of the church's restoration behind.

Francis' new beginnings, as he turned from the physical labour of restoring the fabric of a church building to waiting in the derelict crypt, represent a key shift from church as doing to church as *being*. This warrior-turned-prophet begins again with a conviction of the church as a community of being with a preference for the poor. That is all. A new, global and enduring movement grew out of little more than that conviction and that posture, hidden away in the crumbling remains of the medieval church of the day.

In similar ways the community that we later founded in Poole grew out of a desire to rediscover the *being* of church, the simple gift of Christian community in a particular place. My personal conviction grew from that well-travelled quote from Lesslie Newbigin regarding the nature of the church. He described the church as *the* way in which God has chosen for the gospel to be told and interpreted for every context and every time. He puts it like this: 'The only hermeneutic of the gospel is a congregation of men and women who believe it and live by it.'[4] There is a place, he goes on to say, for the efforts and projects of the church, for mission strategies and courses, conferences and resources, but all of these are secondary to the fundamental *being* of the church at the heart of it all. which is called to live a life that tells the life-giving and transforming nature of the gospel of Jesus.

That was the simple genesis of Reconnect, a community of folk committed to a rhythm of prayer and a Rule of Life which we worked out through prayer and study in our first year together. These practices marked out our commitment to being rather than doing. We did not immediately set out to found projects in our name, raise money and recruit staff. We simply began with the modest ambition of being, as much as we could understand and practically demonstrate, an authentic communal expression of the gospel. We committed to not doing. That is, not allowing 'doing' to shape us and become our fundamental identity. I sensed that many who joined the initial community of Reconnect not only wanted a more authentic expression of Christian community participating in the mission of God, but also wanted to avoid getting exhausted once more by the latest church project. We represented that same group of people that Steve Aisthorpe would later identify through his research as making up perhaps a third of the church. Disciples invisible to the abacuses of the institutional church, but engaged and faithful to the gospel, awaiting expressions of Christian community that might support and nurture their call to a simpler, less frenetic way of being the church.[5] Reconnect drew from that pool perhaps. It has now become established within the family of Anglican churches in Poole, a small but authentic expression of the church finding its place alongside the inherited congregations of the parish system.

It's May and the train has taken me island-hopping from one cathedral outpost to another. First Lincoln, standing sentinel like an ornate lighthouse on fire with the rising sun. Then Ely, a beached liner on the shores of a fenland outcrop, incongruously shipwrecked above the expanse of the flat and windy fields.

Finally Norwich, which has gathered a circular tidal strand of development to its medieval landing, a city rising like the footprint of a puddle, up the hill from the river in all directions. The cathedral origins seem lost in the labyrinth of lanes and streets beyond the station, shy behind its walled-up close, perhaps a little ashamed of what its sacred beginnings have fostered. With all of these cathedrals it's hard to escape the sheer confidence expressed in erecting such dominating buildings on these slivers of land in the midst of almost unhabitable surroundings.

David refuses my willingness to navigate my own way from the curve of the river to the straighter contours of the suburban. As we drive away from the station he quickly gets to storytelling. To his time in San Francisco, slumming it in the dangerous districts of the sprawl of a Californian mega-city to learn from Francis Chan, who has turned his back on the mega-church and embraced the small and the simple.[6] Chan has made something of a countercultural journey in the American church, eschewing the consumerist values and the platform of the church he had planted and starting again with the building blocks of relationship and small community. David is on something of a similar journey and I have come to hear him tell me his story.

On the outside St Alban's church looks like any number of older suburban churches, built as the city escaped the flow and pull of the river and ventured away from the cathedral. It feels like an outpost of the city's ecclesiastical heartlands. The church walls are dressed with large pebbles, like a vertical cobbled street, a beach on display. We find our way in through a back door, past old vestry spaces crammed with the classic clutter of the busy church – sound systems, stacks of chairs, youth resources – to an open space echoing with the burble of children and parents. At the far end, near the old oak entrance doors, a café has been constructed, scaffolding boards making a simple counter from behind which an extremely good Americano and piece of orange polenta cake are produced. This place clearly knows the way to a young Norwich resident's heart.

As a young curate, David was given an opportunity to just

be present and try stuff out in a context where the church was struggling to connect, in this case a large social housing estate in west London. He began, like all good pioneers, by listening. 'I did this flyer called "listening Church", which was like "more tea vicar?"' "Can I just come and ask you what's it like living here? If the church could do one thing for you, what would it be?" And out of that, long story short, we saw eight kids start playing football on the estate.' So not a large church gathering out of nowhere, but a few kids playing football. However, this led to a growing youth work centred on a mothballed school premises that the local authority gave them on a peppercorn rent. This school was then subject to a bid from a large organization promoting transcendental meditation. The fledgling youth club was threatened with eviction. David contacted the local authority and asked what it would take to start a free school there instead. Within three months and with the help of some local primary school teachers a bid was put together that secured the site as a Church of England school, and in so doing enabled the work with young people to continue. David tells me that this experience became a kind of first taste of the eventual pattern of his ministry as a pioneer: 'That made me think maybe in every context, we don't need to wait for the money. We don't need to [sit] around a table saying, "Let's raise a million pounds and do something." It just opened my eyes to what's possible through listening to God, listening to the community, and then taking the first step.'

David tells me this as something of a contrast to the culture of the church movement of which St Alban's is a part. St Alban's has grown out of the initial church plant from Holy Trinity Brompton of St Thomas's in the centre of Norwich. St Alban's is a great example of how larger church plants like St Thomas's, with the resources and momentum behind them from the experience, planning and expertise of HTB, can then go on to plant more innovative expressions of church in other parts of the city. After his surprising journey in west London, David found himself part of the more tried and tested strategy of the resource church network. 'I was really surprised to see how far a small investment in space, a good website, a clear vision, could go. I did a six-week church planting course, we all learnt our elevator pitch and we just set up and people came, lots of them from other churches, but they were hungry for some sort of forward momentum and sense of mission. And we definitely had that.'

But it came with a cost, particularly for those in leadership, who were ambitious for what church planting could do beyond the centre of Norwich, into the suburbs and out into the rural areas of Norfolk. Working with another leader who had also just finished a curacy. David admits there was a naivety involved in the thinking that saw them take on too many church plants too quickly. 'We neither of us had a limit in terms of "let's do it". And so another building and another was just, we were just hungry for that. But eventually it does catch up with you.' The accumulation of plants and buildings involved two new church plants in addition to St Thomas's and St Alban's, a partnership with three other churches, the purchase of a pub and an application to the Church of England's Strategic Development Fund to plant another 10 churches in 5 years. But the centre couldn't hold. David's colleague went off with stress. 'It was just a perfect storm of too much, you know, just way too much too fast, too soon', leaving David as priest in charge of the mother church St Thomas's for two years.

But the experience seems to have shaped David, working at the centre of a growing whirlwind of activity that appears to be based on fruitful experience, on a strategy that 'works' and that promises to hold the solution to the decline of the church and the promise of its renewal. As David describes: 'I guess what was influential for me was seeing a pyramid kind of implode. And being a close part of the top of one of those, but in this whole timeline we'd seen the danger ahead. And it was in 2019 that I went out to San Francisco. I'd been getting this dissatisfaction with the buildings thing. Another service, another congregation, another building. [I'm] thinking 650 buildings or something in Norfolk and we've done three, maybe seven maximum, in seven years. And it costs hundreds of thousands of pounds potentially, which I'm doing as cheaply as possible. It's exhausting.'

Related to our modern culture's misuse of time, Andrew Root explains how the congregations of the western church, immersed as they are in this same culture of acceleration and busyness, sees the expenditure of energy and resources as a necessary good of being the church. It is the nature of organizations in modern western culture to see activity and busyness as a value. If time is no longer held in the fullness of God, stripped of any sense of the sacred and reduced to a resource for our use, then activity, production, efficiency, growth and scale become logical developments. Furthermore, if time is not held within some bigger picture of a purpose for humanity situated somewhere beyond ourselves, then time becomes a series of unrelated units in which good can only mean what can be achieved in any of those moments.

Root refers to this phenomenon within organizations as 'dynamic stabilization'. Dynamic stabilization is shorthand for the effect of the shaping logic of modernity on organizations. Organizations must continually assert their identity and reason for existence through giving out energy and growing (hence dynamic) in order to remain stable. It is no longer something beyond human effort, for example a sense of God's calling or an obedience to God's order as interpreted from the Bible, that gives an organization a sense of its fundamental identity. Decline cannot be seen in any other way except as a threat to the fundamental nature of the organization, so all activity is scrutinized and evaluated against this 'higher good' of stabilization. Will this activity, this project, this initiative bring about growth of the organization and therefore stabilization or not?

For churches the reality of this kind of fundamental value at the heart of society creates a 'double bind'. It is the kind of 'double bind' that I was on the obverse side of when trying to encourage people to engage voluntarily in the community in Acton. It is where the church has to connect with a society built on dynamic stabilization by being the kind of organization that people from that society want to be part of. People in a culture built on busyness as a 'higher good' want to spend time in organizations that are also busy, energetic places. However, in this accelerating world, organizations inevitably compete for the resources and energy that people can give to them. Congregations increasingly find that whereas a generation ago people would come weekly and volunteer regularly to enable programmes and projects to facilitate the life of the church, this has become increasingly hard to achieve. As *Mission-Shaped Church* described very clearly, we are competing with the shopping centre that's now open on a Sunday and the kids' football league that takes place the same morning; but really we are competing for people's energy and time. And there simply aren't enough of those to go round.

Within the logic of 'dynamic stabilization', even as it becomes harder and harder to find the resources to invest in the projects and programmes that are aimed at growth, the drive to provide new and exciting innovation is strong. Novelty and innovation, the new and the fresh, can become proxies for growth and development, for being the kind of organization that people will want to be around and lend their time and energy to. Innovation is suddenly popular. *Mission-Shaped Church* helped create the kind of environment where innovation was no longer looked upon with suspicion but welcomed. However, innovation can become an idol when it is brought into the orbit of 'dynamic stabilization' and used for the purposes of reversing institutional decline. Innovation can easily be seen as a saviour, redeeming the church from its failure to keep up with the pace of society and remain relevant.[7]

Perhaps it's no surprise that leaders, at the pinnacle of this pyramid of activity and innovation, become lightning rods for the exhaustion that is growing. The crash, as David describes it, 'doesn't just suddenly happen. It happens because there's too many supervision meetings that aren't happening, managerial stuff, admin stuff is backed up and financial pressures. All of that kind of thing.' I get a sense of David describing the picture that Andrew Root paints: church leaders entering an impossible vortex of activity because of the internal demands of the logic of 'dynamic stabilization', a merry-go-round that it is impossible to get off without injury; leaders constantly under pressure to produce the next audacious plan, to communicate new vision and fundraise even before the last vision has had a chance to show any fruitfulness; churches in danger of becoming alienated from themselves and the very communities they are seeking to serve as the priorities of the organization supersede the gift of being community together and the slow work of listening and building relationships with others around.

✣

Dancing with the acceleration of modern culture is undoubtedly a massive challenge for the church. The 'double bind' we find ourselves inhabiting is real and difficult to break out of. We will need churches that are busy and activity-oriented places and that engage well with a culture that sees that kind of experience as a good. But our ecclesiology must be built on more than relevance and engagement with the prevailing culture. Our ecclesiology must also hold this in tension with a call to countercultural life, a communal life that demonstrates a prophetic alternative to the displacement and hurry of the world and provides routes back from alienation towards our humanity as beings made in the image of God. The whole church must contain this dialogue between being and doing *within itself*, perhaps in a way that no single church community can. We need one another. And we need to avoid the temptation to see any one church community as the blueprint for the way all churches should be.

I sensed that something of that same tension was at work in St Alban's as a very different kind of church expression from its origins at St Thomas's. What has developed at St Alban's is something of a conversation between the HTB model and the principles of the fresh expression movement. David describes it as a dialogue, a blend between the HTB focus on 'revitalizing a space, working with the building' and 'the fresh expressions methodology and culture, combining the two, because it seemed to me quite often, they're really separate'. The new expression of Christian community there also draws on the story of St Alban, who was converted from his pagan background through the experience of welcoming a Christian priest fleeing from persecution. Alban was so impressed by the priest's faith that he began to join with the priest in his prayers and soon converted to Christianity. Later, when Roman authorities caught wind of the whereabouts of the priest in hiding, they arrived at Alban's door to search the house. Alban dressed himself in the robe and clothing of the priest and presented himself to the authorities.

This story of a non-Christian, an 'outsider' offering hospitality to an 'insider', flipping the common trope of Christian service, acted as a shaping story for the new community emerging at St Alban's. It's a lovely image, the 'pagan' clothing himself in the clothes of the refugee priest, taking on a new identity, standing in bold defiance of the defenders of the prevailing culture. For the new St Alban's this flipped narrative was expressed in creating a space within the building that attempted to blur the standard boundaries of church hospitality and service. It was seeking to create a space and build a mode of community that had space for dialogue and which took a more collaborative posture towards the wider community. 'I didn't want us to be afraid of letting go of a space', David tells me, illustrating their attempts to allow the space to be shaped by the community as much as by the church.

The church building is known as 'Sanctuary'. A word that seemed to sum up a common sense of what the space beyond the walls is for anyone engaging with it. It has become a trusted space as the willingness to let go lent itself to a more open posture toward the community. Sanctuary became a space for a spectrum of activities: jazz, Pilates, prayer, or just hanging out with coffee and conversation. 'Because once people trusted the space then they trusted the idea that the thing you're going to do is like, "Oh, we like Sanctuary. Great we'll come to the Sanctuary".'

In terms of a gathering for worship, what David describes is a centred-set community, a community that at its heart is giving its attention to the worship of Jesus, but whose boundaries are unclear and porous. 'So a good Sunday is where, you know, a window is smashed by the game of football that's happening at the back, while people are having some hopefully really profound prayer experience at the front ... the spirit of it meant that it was family, everyone gets to play, loving family is how we want to run stuff ... we tried to run it with zero rotas, that if you just came early, you would be part of whatever's needed. We tried a lot of things that would break some of the normal ways of being. We didn't have a plan for the year, it was to see what God's doing and join in.'

It's a picture of a community seeking to walk haphazardly in the wake of the Spirit, looking to break the mould of programmes and rotas, flipping the lines of delivery drawn increasingly by the modern culture of activity, and looking to place the messy unpredictability of relationships with God and neighbour as the shaping value of Christian community. Behind the pebbled walls of a nineteenth-century building, a building where the walls are dressed with material carried upstream from the edges of the world around, the horizontal made vertical, the outside a portal to the inside, a church is seeking to escape from the blueprint that might otherwise define it.

There is a church waiting in the spaces like St Alban's. A church that is urgently needed to provide a counterbalancing voice to the scripts of busyness and programmed activity. A church that can lay down paths toward a humanizing community with the grace and being of God at its heart. A church that is content with the wildness and unpredictability of the Spirit. A church that is attentive to the particularities of place, not flattening all the contours of history and context into the kind of cartographies of community that enable us to see only the things that we need for our own survival. A church that can reimagine the stories of its own inheritance as shaping narratives where the Spirit is still at play. A church that can see past, present and future as facets of the fullness of God's time in which the story of salvation is still being told, creating the church in its telling.

Notes

1 Archbishops' Council, *Mission-Shaped Church*.
2 https://freshexpressions.org.uk/ (accessed 8.2.24).
3 Chesterton, *Saint Francis of Assisi*, p. 46.
4 Newbigin, *The Gospel in a Pluralist Society*, p. 227.
5 Aisthorpe, *The Invisible Church*.
6 Chan, *Letters to the Church*.
7 See Root, *The Congregation in a Secular Age*. Root warns that for church leaders innovation can become the 'hypergood of the new'. In other words it is so valued by churches looking to stay relevant in an accelerated culture that they lose sight of the ultimate good of God.

PART 3

Resurrection

'The future is already here,
it's just not very evenly distributed.'

William Gibson

The Farm – A Parable

There was once a farmer who managed a large arable farm on behalf of the owner. The farm was losing money and its future was uncertain.

The farmer invested in the best machinery and used the best fertilizers. The farm was amalgamated with neighbouring farms to reduce costs. The farmer did all these things and worked day and night every day of the year. But the farm continued to lose money.

Then one day the farmer said. 'I know what I will do – I will stop growing crops and I will listen to the land. The land is dying and everything with it. We will work with the land and with the God of creation and see what happens.' And she let the land breathe and allowed herself some rest.

Then the farmer called a meeting to communicate her plans, she sold all the machinery and laid off all the staff. The staff were angry and said the plan was crazy. Other local farmers heard about the plan and shook their heads. Word reached the owner about the plan and he wrote an angry letter saying, 'The farm needs to pay its way!'

Then the farmer said, 'I know what I will do – I will introduce ancient breeds of cattle, horse and pig to graze the grass, and to trim the trees and to till the soil.' These breeds had been largely forgotten but some in the farming community still knew about them. They managed the land naturally and fertilized its soil and life began to return in amazing and surprising ways.

So the land continued to heal. The trees began recovering. Insects returned; butterflies, moths, beetles, bees. Birds began to nest and thrive. The call of the turtle dove was heard once again.

And then the farmer welcomed people onto the land. They walked its paths and sat under its trees, they listened to the birdsong and witnessed clouds of butterflies.

And many of them went home and became like the farmer. They listened to their land and worked with the God of creation. And watched to see what the future brought.

6

Bardney Missional Community, Lincolnshire

It's an early June day but we seem stuck in the past, in early spring or the dampness of last year's autumn, waiting for the season to find its customary rhythm. I am picking my way through a field of grass-covered lumps on the edge of a Lincolnshire farm. It takes a bit of imagination and faith to see the structures that held centuries of communal life, attempting to reconstruct them from all angles, wandering a little foolishly among the mounds of turf. Then there is an angle where the soft peaks of grassed-over stone line up like the breaking of a code and the nave of an ancient monastery takes shape above the cluttered remnants on the ground. Standing where the altar must have been, the pattern of the Christian faith, the cruciform structure of a community and its worshipping life, suddenly maps on the ruins like a key in a lock.

This is Bardney Abbey, a Benedictine monastery founded in the eleventh century, dissolved and abandoned during the sixteenth century in the midst of Henry VIII's wave of dissolution. Now there is nothing but heaps of stone, proving an inconvenience to the industry of the farm through which I have had to walk faithfully, without sign or encouragement, to view this unproductive field on the far fringes of Bardney village. There was a line of monasteries raised up above the Lincolnshire Fens from inland Lincoln to the coast at Boston, like marker buoys in the shallows marking the route out to the deep. These colossal structures of prayer, their communities the cure of sacred time and the souls that depended on it, now seem defeated, laid waste by the triumph of productivity. As if to assert that truth the way to the flattened Abbey is flanked by the gleaming tools of industrial farming, shiny and spikey, ticking with intent in the growing warmth of the sun.

In Bardney village the lonely monastery's irrelevance is increasingly unchallenged by the traditional expressions of its silenced faith. A long narrow oblong of land with what looks like a large wooden shed at the end might be mistaken for an industrial unit, but for the simple cross at the apex. The Catholic church has said its last Mass and the grass has started to grow long on either side of the long straight path toward the chapel. The Methodist congregation has fallen below the threshold where it can be considered a church in its own right, downgraded instead to a class meeting under the auspices of a larger church elsewhere. The Anglican church fares better. However, in the diocese's new hierarchy of parishes, where each parish is encouraged to choose what kind of level of sustainability is realistic for its current life, Bardney has become a community-type church. This means that while they contribute to the costs of the regional staff team, including clergy, the expectation is that the congregation itself will provide all that's needed to maintain its life together.[1] It may be a realistic response to the impossibility of doing the same ministry with less resource, but it leaves St Lawrence's Bardney in no doubt of the fragile position in which it now sits.

Yet the wells of prayer and the centuries of guarding sacred time in the midst of lives forged from the fields and fens of the area nevertheless seem to resist the efforts of secular progress to eliminate them. There was the vicar of St Lawrence's at the beginning of the twentieth century who sought to dig back into time in the fields at the edge of the village. His work resulted in the excavation of many of the dressed stones of the Abbey, the capitals, parts of spiral staircases, and a piecing together of the plan and architecture of the monastery. It became clear, however, that this carved Lincolnshire limestone was not going to survive the elements above the soil, so most of all that was discovered was returned to the earth. The proud monastery resurrected in the imagination of the vicar and his team dissolved back into lumps on the surface of an obscure field. However, some of the best pieces of stone were kept and put on display more recently at the back of the nave of St Lawrence's. As I pick around these illustrated boards, with their pieces of decontextualized stone perched on them, it's tempting to see this as a loud roar of nostalgia at the loss of such a significant place of prayer. But could it also be an exploration of its possible resurrection? A source of reimagination, of remembering? Reforming what has held up the past to reconstruct the future?

☩

When I started out in my leadership of Reconnect, I had high ambitions of what could be achieved in a short space of time. I thought that our commitment to living out the gospel in the midst of our communities and workplaces would be a significant attraction to people. There is no doubt that to some degree that has been the case. People have been drawn to the community, some have found faith among us, and the community has grown. But we remain a relatively small church community. We have got used to feeling fragile and vulnerable, recognizing this as a gift rather than a constant threat. The gift of vulnerability is in the way it holds us in a place of open conversation with the community around us. We do not have the luxury of our size bringing about stability. Nor do we have the challenge of rapid growth or significant size bringing the demands of a large organization which might inevitably draw us inwards to our own concerns.

Our faith in vulnerability and being small took us to the decision to multiply Reconnect into a 'community of communities'. We became four small missional communities, or 'hubs', in different parts of Poole, all in diverse ways seeking to live by a rhythm of prayer and seeking to be a witnessing presence in their local community. In addition to these communities there is also Space for Life, an art and craft group with a Christian 'host team', and other new communities being started by leaders who have come to Poole. Together these existing and emerging communities come within the supportive environment of Poole Missional Communities.[2]

Somewhere on this long journey I embraced the realization that rapid and transformative growth toward something of significant size and impact was a fantasy. The roots of this fantasy lie in all sorts of places, not least my own ego. Stefan Paas argues that one significant part of it lies in a deep-seated nostalgia for the dominance of the church in our society.[3] The point for me is not so much whether God would have us re-Christianize the UK or plant a church in every town in order to reach society. The point is that such a vision and strategy seems to have such a dangerous effect on how we see the place of the church in the mission of God. Is it really all about the church? Is the church as we know it so critical to the future of God's mission that we must seek to revive it at all costs?

As Reconnect developed in its slow and fragile way I began to reflect on whether this was failure or whether God was doing something different. What if we were part of different kind of movement? What if God was bringing about a renewal movement that didn't look like a return to a dominant church in the image we had inherited? What if the move into a secular age, where people were deeply suspicious of organized religion and institutional forms of church yet as spiritually curious as ever, meant that a new, smaller, more vulnerable, more local and more diverse movement of Christian community might connect more fruitfully?

In exploring this question I started to engage with the renewal movements of the past. In reading about the Benedictines, the Beguines, the Franciscans, the Moravians, the Methodists, the Pentecostal movement, two major themes become very evident. First, none of these movements start out by seeking renewal of the current institution. Their leaders may well have lamented the state of the church as an institution, but their response was not to tackle this head on but to focus their attention on God and what he was calling them to do. Second, all these movements begin on the edge or the outside of their contemporary system. Whether it be in the desert of Egypt, the cellar of a disused church in Assisi, in exile, in homes, among the poor and the outcasts, the Spirit of renewal works at the edge. The Spirit draws leaders of renewal to edge places, into spaces where something new can explore soil and take root, and from where a movement can grow which in time (often a very long time) impacts the whole environment.

✠

Someone put a book into my hands as a gift a few years ago. The book was *Wilding* by Isabella Tree.[4] *Wilding* tells the story of the Knepp Estate in Sussex, which in the year 2000 embarked on a remarkable project to rewild. Arable farming was ditched, staff made redundant, equipment sold off and the land left to nature. It's a story about how the land was renewed and regenerated in extraordinary and surprising ways, by doing very little except listen, learn, enable and observe.

As I read I realized that the story that Tree was telling had resonances with the story and predicament of the church in the UK. What insights, I wondered, might there be from Knepp and other such projects? Are these insights that we might want to pay attention to in the landscape of the ministry and mission of the church struggling to find its way in a secular age?

In *Wilding* Isabella Tree describes how at Knepp the standard intensive farming methods were failing. The farm was losing money. Amalgamating with neighbouring farms to try and create economies of scale didn't work. The marginal land they were on simply did not supply the kind of yields necessary to make this kind of farming sustainable. Stopping was a tough decision. Others advocated one more throw of the dice. But the brave decision was made to stop and be open to new ways of managing the land.

Intensive wheat farming had blinded those farming the Knepp estate to the reality that this was very marginal land for that kind of farming. Once they stopped, they began to listen more intently to the land. In doing so the land began to reveal its past and to disclose some of the resources and heritage that were part of its unique nature. Oak trees some 300 years old, that stood dying at the centre of heavily farmed wheat fields, were symbols of an ecology that was being ignored and ravaged by the way the land was being used. Listening to the land proved to be the beginnings of a route towards a new vision for the way the land could be managed productively and sustainably. Such listening is the basis of pioneering ministry. But the story of Knepp also drove home the critical connection between listening and surrender. It's all too easy to listen with our strategies for the future already inked on to the plans in our pockets. To truly listen is to listen with an openness and abandonment to the surprise of the Spirit and to the clues of the future written in the history and geography of a place.

The process of listening to the land led the Knepp estate to introduce free-ranging grazing animals into the estate. These mimicked the roles that ancient herbivores of the past had played, much like the reintroduced wolves in Yellowstone that had brought about a 'trophic cascade' of natural adaptations and changes in the ecology of the park.[5] The introduction at Knepp of these 'keystone species' started to have an extraordinary effect on the ecology of the estate. Biodiversity exploded in a very short space of time. Dung beetles became plentiful again, nightingales recolonized the area, clouds of the purple emperor butterfly could be witnessed in the tops of the oak tree woods, white storks have been reintroduced and successfully raised their young.

What is distinctive about the process of wilding is the different relationship set up between human organization and nature. Conservation tends to manage environments for certain rare or declining species. Wilding on the other hand is an emergent process. Isabella Tree calls her book *Wilding* because she is keen to point out that wilding is a forward-looking, surprising process. Rewilding implies a return to some previous wild state. A process that might be more like restoration than renewal. Time and time again the estate at Knepp threw up some profound surprises as the renewal, return and colonization of different kinds of species constantly outran the experts' predictions.

The story of the Knepp estate might be read as a parable for the church in the UK. We use methods that in many contexts are nor fruitful or sustainable, and others which are resource intensive and programmatic. We are amalgamating parishes in the hope of sustaining what we do. Yet in many ways we too are farming in old ways on land that is now marginal, and we need to stop and listen deeply to our context. When our machines have stopped and the dust settled we may just be able to discern the nature of the soil at our feet.

Where this is happening, people are rediscovering the 'keystone species' of the church – the apostles, the prophets and evangelists who have been marginal in our church life for so long. They are being reintroduced and are bringing a renewed diversity. A diversity that is surprising and which confounds and challenges our assumptions about the nature of church.

And it is wilding, not rewilding, that we must seek. The wild Spirit of God is not a utility to be employed for the purposes of nostalgia. Wilding invites humans to be facilitators of a vision of nature, or of the Spirit. A vision with a future orientation replete with surprise. Our role is as enablers, curators and observers. We say, 'Yes, that's a nightingale, but we never expected it to breed there.' Or, 'Yes, that's church, but we never expected it to look like that!'

※

Pete Atkins and I have met before. After my first visit he had given me a stone which sits on my desk at home and which was chosen from a numbered collection of stones dug from the earth of the grounds of his converted seventeenth-century barn in Bardney. Each stone has been prayed over and represents someone with a heart and vision for the renewal of the church in one of the counties of the UK. Out of the sediments and layers of the Christian history of this place Pete and his wife Kath, and their missional community based here, draw inspiration for the renewal of the church here and beyond.

So the story of the beginnings of Bardney Missional Community is a story I have heard Pete tell me before, but I urge him to tell me again. Pete and Kath felt led by the Spirit to purchase a dilapidated agricultural barn in the village of Bardney in order to live there and begin a community founded on prayer. They sensed they would need somewhere big enough to include a dedicated space for prayer and so set about converting the barn towards this vision. The barn needed surveying before any work was carried out and the surveyor warned Pete that it would be incredible if the foundations were viable after centuries of deterioration in the wet ground of Lincolnshire. But to everyone's amazement the foundations turned out to be sound. What was the material down there that was making this barn so unusually resistant to subsidence over time? Pete set about digging down to find out and what he discovered was remarkable. 'The treasure we found was that the entire building, the foundations of the entire building, are made from the stone from the mediaeval monastery. So it's mostly eleventh–twelfth-century carved Lincolnshire limestone,' Pete says. 'We found an amazing foundation to this particular building, which no one knew before.'

The refounding of the barn on the foundations of the history of Bardney acted as a prophetic call, an invitation from the Spirit, to refound a community of prayer in this village of historic prayer and Christian community. As Pete describes it: 'It was like, the stones here meant that there was a monastic community in the past, and "they're here for you, because we want you to build on that tradition for the future".'

So the converting of the barn, and a series of old stables associated with it, was shaped by that vision to found a life on prayer and community in the tradition of the monastic communities of Bardney. What has developed since then is a community centred on a daily rhythm of prayer and a weekly rhythm of gathered worship in the barn. From that foundation the community has followed the Spirit into the community of Bardney, beginning with a monthly tea hosted in the barn that has now outgrown the barn and moved into the village hall. Mission has developed through listening, serving and building community but as much as anything else through surprising invitations that have led the community down unplanned paths. This has included the provision of two shop units, which after two years of prayer and community consultation have been converted into a community café. Through the relationships that have developed with people in the village, with people finding faith and others drifting into the village from elsewhere and joining the prayer rhythm, the missional community has grown.

At St Lawrence's in the village I discover that the church is built on land gifted during the time of the Benedictine monastery. It was gifted in order to build a place of worship for the villagers who were starting to frustrate the monks by being too rowdy and ill-disciplined when joining in with worship at the monastery. It's not a great origin story for the parish church. I'm told they are less disruptive now! However, it does touch on something that may surprise us: in many ways the monastery *was* the local church, in which the local people were both participants and at times spectators. Charles Taylor describes the tension in medieval society between the aspiration of all to a life of Christian devotion and the reality of day-to-day to life for the majority. 'We could describe it,' Taylor writes, 'as lying between the demand to love God, which means to follow him to the cross, to be ready to renounce everything, on one hand; and the demand to affirm ordinary human life and flourishing, on the other.'[6] In the medieval age this tension was held in a relaxed kind of way in a 'hierarchical complementarity', in other words a recognition that some were called to the 'higher' vocations of monastic or priestly ministry and others to the vocations in 'ordinary life' within an order of society that complemented one another. This compromise could be summarized in the formula: 'The clergy pray for all, the lords defend all, the peasants labour for all.'[7]

Taylor argues that part of the zeal of the Reformers lay in resolving this tension by lifting everyone to the level and standard of those who have given up everything to live a life of piety and prayer. Protestantism, he argues, works toward 'attempting to raise general standards, not satisfied with a world in which only a few integrally fulfil the gospel, but trying to make certain pious practices general'.[8] For Taylor part of the story of secularism is a rejection of this demand within western society, a collapse of this tension not upwards into universal piety and gospel faithfulness, but downwards towards a general rejection of the gospel and its call to a life faithful to God.

It's hard to see how to hold the tension between gospel faithfulness and a flourishing life in the brokenness of the world. Many of the attempts at levelling up toward faithfulness have resulted in joyless regimes of moral rule-keeping and rote religious devotion. It's hardly any wonder that secularism took root in western society as people felt that the Reformers' project had run its course and voted against it not just with their feet but with their souls and bodies. Yet in the uneasy tension between pious monks and rowdy villagers, in their newly-built church, there was a way in which the reality of the demands of daily life and the desire for God could be held together.

The loss of the monastic strand in the Protestant church has given us a more monochrome church, unplugged from this life-giving movement and its integrated practices of spiritual devotion constantly seeking to attend to the fullness of God's time in the midst of the world. Time and time again the monastic strand brings a renewing impetus to the ailing energies of the congregational strand. 'During a lengthy period of time,' the American missiologist Ralph Winter writes, 'perhaps a thousand years, the building and rebuilding of modalities was mainly the work of the sodalities. That is to say the monasteries were uniformly the source and vitality that flowed into the diocesan side of the Christian movement. We think of the momentous Cluny reform, then the Cistercians, then the Friars and finally the Jesuits – all of them strictly sodalities, but sodalities that contributed massively to the building and the rebuilding of the *Corpus Cristianum*, the network of dioceses, which Protestants often identify as "the" Christian movement.'[9]

Within the historical decoupling and coupling of this long tension, it's fascinating, then, to begin to explore the nature of the community emerging at Bardney, particularly given Pete's approach, which is deliberately relaxed on structure and open to the wildness of the Spirit. The community that has emerged from the establishment of a rhythm of prayer and an openness to the Spirit's leading into the community is not a 'church plant' in the traditional way we have come to understand it. As Pete explains: 'Most of the team are not part of the local churches.' Yet at the same time they are hugely engaged with the life of the inherited congregations of the area, working together on Lent courses, community events and Christian festivals throughout the year. 'You've got a genuine mixed ecology here,' he says, which develops the uneasy dialogue between the congregational/diocesan strand and the monastic strand into something more complex, more wild.

☩

Over the last 30 years one Canadian plant biologist has single-handedly and radically transformed our understanding of the ecology of forests. Suzanne Simard grew up in the temperate rain forests of British Columbia and was insatiably curious about the mysteries of the forest all around her. Her work as a scientist went on to develop a robustly researched reframing of the nature of the forest as a complex symbiosis between trees and the vast network of fungal filaments coursing through the soil. Trees are not stand alone, solitary organisms competing for light and nutrients in the soil around them. Forests are communities where ancient 'mother trees' seed and nurture their offspring through the underground fungal networks that act as a vast exchange system for nutrients between trees. Furthermore, the fungal network enables trees to 'talk' to one another, to give and receive chemical messages, for example of warning or distress, to which trees can respond by delivering nutrients to other trees in the network. The forest is a 'wood wide web'.[10]

Simard's work helps us cross the boundaries created by a particularly reductive and rational way of thinking which sees a forest as a collection of individual static units. The church stands on a similar horizon, wondering if its way of seeing the church as a model, as a thing standing almost outside of time and place, might be equally reductive. Maybe the church could be a forest? Maybe church is not one gathered congregation to which we give our time and energy, affiliate our membership and lend our credit card details. Maybe it's something more like life within an ecosystem of Christian society, where a complex variety of expressions of Christian community guard and nurture the identity of the body of Christ in a way that no one community can. The full identity and the fullness of the body of Christ is the sum of this vast ecosystem. Its unity is somehow 'in-between' and within the diverse conversations across the networks of mutual support and nurture.

Might we therefore see the trees and their associated fungal networks as a metaphor for the nourishing symbiosis between the congregational/diocesan and monastic that, as Winter argues, is the fundamental nature of the church. It is not that one is more ecclesial than the other, with the monastic an adjunct, perhaps the more overtly missional 'wing' of the true church. Rather, the church *is this dialogue*, the interrelating. It's in the dialogue, or better still conversation, between the polarities of congregation and monastic in time and place that the church is made known by the Spirit.

Pete and his team attempt to illustrate this with the metaphor of boats and harbours, where boats represent communities embedded in places where they live a life of prayerful witness, and harbours represent the gathered points of communal worship and spiritual sustenance. 'I do feel that the picture of small boats and harbours helps us really understand what I think we're aiming for. Which is that there are living communities in every place and every network where it's not difficult to find Jesus basically. And where he is accessible through his people and through what those people are doing whatever aspect of the Kingdom they're involved in at the time, from a food bank to a worship time, to the healing of the sick to caring for people in the hospital ... wherever you find the Kingdom.'

This is a vision profoundly conscious of the deep foundations in time and place on which it is building. 'We have founded a prayer-based community, we would love those foundations to be in place for hundreds of years, well beyond us, like the previous monastery, it wasn't a quick thing. It had deep foundations in prayer for a long time.'

Pete, Kath and the community at Bardney are venturing into a new landscape, a new paradigm, much like Isabella Tree and her husband and team did at Knepp. It's a paradigm open to surprise and mystery and the leading of the Spirit, where form and structure, survival and stabilization are not as primary as the being of God and the relationships with one another. 'He's asked us to cross an unfamiliar landscape ... When we get to wherever we're getting to, then a new church will arise, which will hopefully not stop, it will keep moving ... We need to travel more lightly. And I think he has a new future for us. And it's a future that is described better by the relational, doing life together, God at the heart of it, God present being led by the Spirit kind of a way.'

John V. Taylor argued: 'Our theology would improve if we thought more of the church being given to the Spirit than of the Spirit being given to the church.'[11] This argument summarizes succinctly the paradigm shift invited by the Spirit, to one where we trust in God to continually make the church in the wake of the Spirit's movement in the world. Rather than structures, Pete describes a set of values, based fundamentally on a trust in the sustaining presence of God, which guides and shapes the life and work of the community. 'We talk about a candle, a table and a door. So the candle for us is the presence of God, Father, Son, and Spirit. The table is about community life, family, learning sometimes about welcoming the stranger to the table of hospitality, and the door is about the welcome in and the sending out in mission. So it's simple, it's God Himself, community life, and mission, [which] are going to sustain life for these communities.'

I wander through the village again and down towards the River Witham, which drains sluggishly across the flatness of the Fens toward the north sea at Boston. This was a major route for transport and commerce in the days of the monasteries. These centres of prayer integrated into the contours of the landscape, the river, the sea, trade and agriculture, time and place. Now roads, direct and straight, slice across the drained fens like an engineering diagram, contradicting the lie of the land, the threat of the invading sea, the once forever-flooded fields. We have dominated the landscape, found ways of draining it, excavating it of its life, always assuming that the land will sustain us from the fathomless mine of its resources, believing that there will always be more to sate our hungry industry.

What is left of the monasteries lie like the worthless rubble of our mining at the edges of fiercely productive fields, scattered remnants on the surface of our thinning soils. Yet their roots go deep. Within the dry ground at the foot of a stunted pillar of a dead Abbey, strands of subterranean life, thought abandoned to another time, another world, wait in the dark. Invisible spores float on the currents of memory, history, tradition, on the four winds of the Spirit, carrying ancient codes of renewal for another age.

There must be patience and there must be darkness for a spore to nudge the soil and emerge into life. Perhaps it has lain there silently for a century, perhaps an age, until the ground is shaken and time finds a fullness, a place in which the vital connections are made. But 'the Lord is not slow in keeping his promise, as some understand slowness'.[12] There will be a sustaining from the depths of the ground. For God was in the ground three days and with God 'a day is like a thousand years and a thousand years are like a day'.[13]

Notes

1 For more info and analysis of Lincoln Diocese's strategy for parish ministry see https://www.churchtimes.co.uk/articles/2022/18-march/features/features/retrenchment-and-survival-one-diocese-s-response-to-the-crisis (accessed 8.2.24).

2 www.poolemc.org.uk (accessed 8.2.24).

3 Paas (2016), *Church Planting in the Secular West*, pp. 96–101;

Paas (2019), *Pilgrims and Priests: Christian Mission in a Post-Christian Society*, pp. 68–86.

4 Tree (2018), *Wilding*.
5 https://education.nationalgeographic.org/resource/wolves-yellowstone (accessed 8.2.24).
6 Taylor (2007), *A Secular Age*, p. 80.
7 Taylor, p. 45.
8 Taylor, p. 82.
9 Winter (1974), 'The two redemptive structures of God's mission'. This seminal research paper is widely available as a pdf download on the internet. Winter used the term modality (from the word mode, that is, what is customary or the normal way things are) for the congregational form and sodality (from the Latin word *sodalis*, which refers to a group of people with a strong sense of belonging and common purpose to which they have made a commitment) for the monastic form.
10 Simard (2022), *Finding the Mother Tree*.
11 Taylor (1972), *The Go-Between God*, p. 133.
12 2 Peter 3.9.
13 2 Peter 3.8.

7

Garden Church, Great Melton, Norfolk

It's autumn in Norfolk and the skies have been heralding the annual revolution that is the coming of winter. Huge skeins of clamouring geese have been arriving across the expanse of the North Sea and settling on the flooded fields between the dunes and farmland of the coast. I'm also heading home but make a detour to take in the village of Great Melton. It's not immediately clear in what way Great Melton is 'great'. It is certainly not a comment on its size. I drive through in both directions before realizing that the short line of large houses set back from the road is the village. Just beyond it lies an impressively well-resourced cricket club and not far from that lies Great Melton church, tucked away on the corner of a lane disappearing into the fields.

The church grounds hold the existing parish church and adjacent to it the ghost of another. Only a stone's throw from the main church, among the gravestones and yew trees, another tower stands, marks on one side evidence of a roof and nave long disappeared. Until the early eighteenth century Great Melton was a 'divided parish' with two separate buildings serving congregations from two manor estates. The parish boundary passed through the gap between the two buildings! The two parishes were eventually brought together into one with one building providing the place of worship and the other falling into dereliction. Surprisingly, it was today's working building that by the 1860s was falling into disrepair, with worship taking place next door. Yet it was the former church building that was rebuilt with the material from the latter. All that now remains of this previous church is the duplicate tower.

I wonder what differences existed in our culture in the 1860s that we could be so apparently pragmatic about our heritage in order to make way for new developments. Would we do that now? Would we fall into two opposing parties each campaigning for the merits of our own particular building? This of course is no idle thought experiment. No less passionately-held convictions are being tested here as the church continues to find its way into the future. For Great Melton is now playing host to one of a growing network of small church communities called Garden Church. On the church notice board a regular 'Garden Church' is advertised as part of the monthly rhythm of parish services. Garden Church, however, does not take place in the church building but in the cricket pavilion back up the lane towards the village.

GARDEN CHURCH, GREAT MELTON, NORFOLK

As we emerge from the pandemic I keep coming across movements of networked small communities, not dissimilar from Poole Missional Communities. Some of these movements have been going for years, others are just getting started. Perhaps the digital exposure created by the pandemic brought these networks of small communities to greater attention. Perhaps the deepening conversation about the future of the church, accelerated by the experience of Covid, has brought the voice of these movements more into the open. One such movement is Garden Church, which was started by David Lloyd, the leader of St Alban's in Norwich. I had spoken to David about this movement when I visited him in Norwich. He encouraged me to meet Charlotte, who leads the 'Garden' in Great Melton.

Charlotte is a young mum who had been brought up in the village, moved away to university, grown in faith, and then returned. There remains a strong commitment in her to the parish of Great Melton. She still attends on Sundays, sings in the choir, volunteers as a church warden. She is most definitely 'of this parish'. It was when Charlotte had her first child, however, that the pragmatic challenges of worshipping at the parish church really began to press on her. 'I was really confused because I always felt really drawn back to the tradition I was in, and I'm in Great Melton church, and I was the only young person there. So I didn't really know what to do. And two years ago, I had a little girl, my first child. And I thought I've got to move churches, because how can I bring, I can't bring her here? There's no toilet, I can't change her nappy here. You know, there's nothing here.'

Through a mutual connection Charlotte met David Lloyd, who was beginning to experiment with small and simple gatherings of people for worship in villages and other contexts around Norfolk. The concept of Garden Church immediately fired Charlotte's imagination. It put form to something that had been growing within her dis-ease about the way in which her church community functioned. It provided a positive practical response to a latent desire she had had for years to experience a more communal, participative church. 'It's opened people's eyes to rediscovering what it might mean to do church and what church looks like ... and it's the same for me.' So having at first hoped for St Thomas's to lend Great Melton a vicar or some musicians, Charlotte changed tack and agreed to step into the role of leader of the Garden Church.

Talking to David Lloyd it's hard to get a handle on the exact moment that Garden Church started. There was little strategy or fanfare, no big launch party, but a seed took root in David's own garden and a group began to gather. That seed grew and multiplied. When I talk to David only two years later there are 14 'Gardens' meeting across Norfolk, most in rural villages.

Garden Church is not a model. There is nothing complex about it. It is a stripping back to the simplicity of church as a set of relationships, to God in Christ, to one another and to the wider community. It's a stripping back in terms of size and complexity and effort. Charlotte describes the practice of Garden Church as a renewal of the simple practices of 'people gathering, sharing food, sharing stories, becoming family, praying together, reading Scripture together'. 'There is space', she says, 'for everyone to use their gifting should they want to or should they wish to and it's encouraged and valued.' David refers to this as 'rediscipling the disciples'. A movement from membership to community. From attendance to participation. From growth to multiplication. From programmes to patience.

People are finding Garden Church from a variety of backgrounds, ages, traditions and for a variety of reasons. There are some who are not neurotypical, those in particular with ADHD who have found a larger congregation too difficult. There are some burnt out by long-term service in a more traditional context. Others struggling to make the connections between the Christian communal life of the New Testament and formal worship at a local parish church. A lady who is the organist at the local parish, another who has been church warden for 17 years. As David acknowledges, the Garden is finding its locus on the edges with exiles and dissidents from the decline of traditional forms of church in a secular age. 'I sense this post-Christendom, post-congregational thing is much bigger than we might dare to imagine. Everyone's hammering away at running Sunday and that needs to keep happening, but most of our resources go into that and we found with the Garden just a load of people sensing, feeling and being like nowhere or being in a liminal space or being just in a different place.' There are also a growing group of people engaging with Garden who are new to faith, for whom something small and relational is not a consumer choice but a natural expression of Christian life among the people they already relate to.

That said, the relationship with the inherited church is more complex than might be assumed at first. This is not sectarian church planting with the arrogance that is often associated with that, a conviction of some sort of vision for the true church. Many of those making Garden their church remain committed to their local parish church. Others are coming to Garden within a whole personal menu of engagement with different local expressions of church and Christian spirituality. This is not about planting better churches. There is a movement being generated which seems to be opening up something that widens the diversity of expressions of Christian community and worship. They are not in competition with local established expressions of church, in most cases they are existing alongside, and are careful not to be a source of friction within the wider ecology of the local church. Charlotte describes Garden as an extension 'in addition to the building' of the parish – 'it's not excluding the [traditional parish] church'. 'It's got to bring unity, not disunity,' says David. 'We're not trying to sectarian plant. We're not trying to be like we've got it right, you've got it wrong. We want it to be a catalyst for local growth and revitalization.'

But in what sense is Garden Church missional? Is it not simply a reframing of the existing church? Just a redistribution of those already committed to the Christian faith into smaller, informal gatherings in more local settings? That might well be something to be welcomed and celebrated. But the question remains how these small communities are relating to the particular place in which they are meeting. Certainly in terms of activity there is little mission going on. There is an honest concern not to tread on the toes of longstanding local churches and the mission they are already engaged in. There is also a deliberate retreat from the notion of mission as doing: 'its not running holiday Bible studies' or 'running an event that we can tick a box and say, we've done some mission'. Rather, it is giving attention to the missional quality of people's lives, as individuals but most importantly as communities. The mission of Garden Church is in the nature of their life as family, as welcoming community. Charlotte describes it quite simply as 'a really comfortable place for everyone to be'. David describes their mission as 'less like, "get busy running events" and more "we'll model a Garden and grow in character and do life well" … it's quite underwhelming, it's not very busy. But it's bearing fruit.'

There's a naivety with Garden Church, a childlike playfulness that is the experience of having jettisoned so much of the heaviness of a way of being the church that seems so weighed down by strategies and theorems, models and methods. There is the constant experience of surprise that is surely one of the authentic signs of the work of the Spirit. These are communities playing in the wake of a move of the Spirit, liberated from any sense that this technique or this programme has been the key to success, or will be in the future.

The story of the phenomenal growth of the early church has often been mined for forgotten or neglected elements that might cure the current malaise of the western church. As we sense and experience the collapse of the certainties and common assumptions of Christendom, many increasingly look to the pre-Constantinian era for insight into our own age. In the study of the early church it's possible perhaps to see two narratives that explain the phenomenal growth of this Messianic Jewish movement. One story goes that the genesis story of the movement, the explosion into life of the early church at Pentecost, is *the* explanatory narrative for the expansion of Christianity into the Greco-Roman world. This is the 'white hot faith'[1] at the heart of the movement which can only be explained by the coming of the Holy Spirit that turns a timorous group of despairing followers of a dead Messiah into anointed and fearless ambassadors of the gospel of Jesus Christ.

The other story is a sociological one, which argues that the growth of the early church can be explained by a study of the numbers involved and the social circumstances within which the growth occurred. This new Christian community certainly 'turned the world upside down'[2] in ways that were deeply attractive to many people in the harsh and stratified world of the Roman Empire. Ronald Stark's research into the early centuries of the church provides a number of examples of the way in which this new social phenomenon was deeply attractive to those treated harshly and discriminately by the Roman system. Women in particular found in the Christian community a radical experience of dignity and compassion. Perhaps the plagues that affected Roman cities in those centuries proved to be pivotal events in the growth of the church. The Christian communities' eternal perspective gained traction in this context. But it was also their practical care and compassion that had a deep impact on the pagan population of the time. Whereas most citizens who were able to do so would flee to the fresh air of the hills surrounding the cities when any hint of plague arrived, leaving the sick to die, Christians would stay, caring not only for the sick of their own community but those of their non-Christian neighbours as well. The effect was twofold. First, survival rates among the Christian community were higher, children and women of childbearing age were surviving the waves of plague and the Christian population consequently grew, proportionately and ultimately in number. But second, the witness of the Christian community, their courage and compassion in the face of the horrors of pandemics was hard to ignore. Here was the Christian gospel written in the lives of Christians caring for friends and neighbours, which for many proved decisive in their decision to join this community.[3]

In a similar way Alan Kreider argues that the growth of the early church can't be easily explained by an extrapolation of the Book of Acts. For one thing growth varied a great deal from place to place, with large numbers of Christians in North Africa for example, while certain cities remained almost completely without any Christian presence. But for another, while the growth of Christianity is clear, it grew despite laws against it, social convention ill-disposed to it and persecution a common and frequent experience. So why did it grow? Kreider's answer is to be found in what the early church leaders wrote about. 'According to the evidence at our disposal, the expansion of the churches was not organized, the product of a mission programme; it simply happened. Further growth was not carefully thought through. Early Christian leaders did not engage in debates between rival "mission strategies".'[4] But what they were concerned about, judging by the amount that was written about it, was the virtue of "patience". Kreider tells us: 'The Christians wrote treatises on patience – three of them – but they did not write a treatise on evangelism.'[5]

Kreider puts the growth of the early Christian church down to a commitment to the virtue of patience. What patience summarized theologically for the early Christians was faith in Christ who had already entered time and transformed our understanding of it into something eternally held by the Father in heaven. Time was God's. God was in control and they were not. The role of the church was not to capture time and use it for its own advancement; this would be to put the Christian community in the place that God had already shown them to be God's alone. Instead, the role of the church was to live in the time and place that they were but in the light of eternity. They were to live as if eternity was a reality now and for all time. They were to live as those with faith in sacred time. The church was a 'patient ferment', a slowly developing presence of Christian communal life in the midst of Roman society, bubbling away slowly and discreetly, gradually transforming the world in which it lived.

If we are looking for a magic ingredient from the life of the early church, patience makes a good candidate. Because patience is rooted in the character of God. Patience is essentially putting the sovereignty of God's time, of sacred time, as the rhythm and structure of our own lives. It is participating in the life of God at a pace that is the pace of love. And this is the pace that Jesus demonstrated was the pace of the life of the Father, as Kosuke Koyama described so beautifully in his book *Three Mile an Hour God*. Jesus came out of the wilderness where 'our speed is slowed down until gradually we come to the speed on which we walk – *three miles an hour*' (p.5). And Jesus walked the roads and tracks of Judea and Galilee with a patience and pace that never seemed to be hurried, that always waited for the souls and bodies of those he met to come alongside him. And so Koyama argues:

> Love has a speed. It is an inner speed. It is a spiritual speed. It is a different kind of speed from the technological speed to which we are accustomed. It is 'slow' yet it is lord over all other speeds since it is the speed of love. It goes on in the depth of our life, whether we notice it or not, whether we are currently hit by a storm or not, at three miles an hour. It the speed we walk and therefore it is the speed the love of God walks.[6]

Can we really do life at walking pace, though? To be in the world, and with the world, surely makes walking at three miles an hour impossible. There were times when Jesus was incredibly busy, times when he seemed to rush from one encounter to another, he was anything but slow. John Swinton acknowledges this point, but he says, 'Koyama's point is that three miles an hour is the *average* speed that Jesus walked at. Moving faster is not the norm.'[7] The testimony of the gospels is of a Jesus for whom slowness is the pace at which the truth of love and grace can be revealed and embraced by others. In the gentle and patient ways in which he comes alongside others, walks with them, turns aside for them, makes a detour for them, allows them to follow him without fully understanding him, he demonstrates that 'God goes slowly in his educational process'[8] with people. And so Swinton invites us to become 'friends of time', of God's time. A time that is 'a way of being in the fullness of time that is not determined by productivity, success, or linear movements toward personal goals. It is the way of love, a way of the heart.'[9]

With Garden Church the lack of busyness may well be a reaction to the intense busyness of some of the churches that those joining have experienced. But it does also mirror the embracing of God's time that was the 'patient ferment' of the early church. It mirrors that commitment first and foremost to the being of God, the being of Christian community which is a gift of God, to relationships which can only grow and develop at the speed of love. Which is why the expressed desire to come alongside and be with the inherited church, as friends and co-workers in the growing ecology of the Kingdom, and not to go faster than the existing local church, is consistent with this priority of patience. And it's mirrored in the experience of David as a leader whose role seems one of gently creating the environment in which this movement continues to grow through the power of the Spirit. As he describes: 'So I'm seeing 90% wonder and 10% effort, the previous eight years I felt I saw maybe 90% effort and 10% wonder. And that's very humbling, and quite exciting.'

The science of complex systems argues that there are thresholds within the disequilibrium of these systems that when reached can tip systems into rapid reorganization into a new structure. Often the seeds of this new structure have been within the system before. They exist as ideas, or memories, or they have come into the system from conversation and engagement with the wider environment and have been gaining a following, a traction, within the system for a time. These new ideas, or 'attractors' in the language of some complexity theorists, are the principles and values that a system organizes and shapes itself around. They are resisted by the system for a time. The natural order of a system is to protect its stability and it will resist new information or ideas that threaten that stability. But there comes a point where the disequilibrium being experienced by the system, through changes in the external environment, reaches a tipping point. It is threshold events that can tip systems into a new paradigm of organization. Events like thunderstorms in the desert, suddenly causing dormant seeds to germinate, take root and bloom, transforming the landscape into a rage of colour. Is the Covid pandemic such an event for the church? And if so, is Garden Church and other new expressions of church simply a reframing by social pressures of the existing church into a new shape?

In which case do you have to choose between two ways of making sense of new church movements – be they the Benedictines, the Franciscans, the Methodists movement or Garden Church – that they are either movements of the Spirit or constructions of the social context? The reality I believe is more complex. If we only see church as a noun, as a thing, a model or an organization, we will always find it easy to explain the church in social terms. But if we see the church more as a verb, as something that happens when people in a particular time and place encounter Jesus and form communities around that experience, the church becomes something that emerges as the sum of these encounters, experiences and relationships. Rowan Williams describes it like this in the foreword to the *Mission-Shaped Church* report:

> The church is what happens when people encounter the risen Jesus and commit themselves to sustaining and deepening that encounter in their encounter with each other. There is plenty of theological room for diversity of rhythm and style, so long as we have ways of identifying the same living Christ at the heart of every expression of Christian life in common.[10]

The church is something that emerges from the work of the Spirit in a particular time and place, a particular context. In which case we would expect it to be influenced by the particular social and organizational forms of the context on which the church is placed. But this is not purely a social construction. We do not have to choose. Rather, in between the conversations taking place within the church, with the testimony of Scripture and with tradition and between the church and its context, the Holy Spirit is at work making connections, forming and reforming the church. This is why John V. Taylor called the Holy Spirit the 'go-between God'. Because primarily the role of the Spirit is to help us to see the other and to enable relationship; 'it is always he who gives one to the other and makes each really see the other'.[11] The Holy Spirit is a mediator present and active in the midst of an ongoing conversation between the church, its past and present, the messy reality of the world and the future that is the ultimate destiny of history, the fullness of the Kingdom of God.

I was given a book last Christmas called *Fifty Words for Snow*. Riffing on the famous adage about the eskimo language and snow, the book offers 50 examples of words for snow or snow-related features from cultures across the globe. We learn for example that the Greenlandic word *immiaq* means both 'melted ice or snow' or 'beer'. This is because melted snow was the source of drinking water for any travelling hunter. When people began importing beer to Greenland in the 19th century there was really only one word for something you drink – so *immiaq* became the word for beer.[12]

Language is as fluid and fickle as the cultures in which words emerge and where they travel through. Language is effortlessly creative as new words emerge, fuse, are adapted and reappropriated to keep up with the demands of our experience.

There are good reasons from science why we might have so

many words for snow. Snow is a various, fickle thing too. Each chapter of *Fifty Words for Snow* is prefaced by an image from the nineteenth-century photographer and mineralogist Wilson Bentley. Bentley perfected a technique for photographing snowflakes. He then spent the next 50 years doing it. And in 1933 his extraordinary photographs were compiled into one book, *Snow Crystals*. In the book there are 2,453 different images of a single snow crystal. And every single one is unique! Leafing through this book is a spiritual exercise in wonder, as your narrow concept of snow is whipped up into a blizzard of complexity, beauty and diversity.[13]

However, we might learn something from the snowflake photography of Wilson Bentley to help widen our imagination of what we might mean when we utter the word 'church'. Because what Bentley's technical ingenuity and skill was able to reveal to us was something about the nature of snow. For snowflakes are also an *emergent phenomena*. Their particular form is an unpredictable result of a process of self-organization from a lower level of complexity to another. Snowflakes form from water vapour when a threshold in the air temperature is reached, at which point the water molecules self-organize into crystalline structures. These crystals all share a common basic six-sided structure. However, the particular conditions and journey of that snowflake's formation and fall to earth shapes (literally) the individual snowflake into a unique pattern.

So what we blandly call 'snow' is in fact this unbelievably diverse and complex collection of forms which are the unique consequence of their own particular set of conditions and journeys. History and context are written into each flake. With enough knowledge and experience you can read back from a snowflake's form and say with some certainty the kind of conditions in which it was formed. Snowflakes 'carry their history on their backs'.

And much like the word 'snow', which at least in the UK has a kind of dull, normative meaning, the word 'church' could do with a piece of illuminating work not unlike the photographs of Wilson Bentley. We may experience the diversity, breadth and creative scope of the church – but our language struggles to stretch to accommodate it.

But further, the emergent nature of snowflakes give us an insight into the nature of other kinds of reality. Human organizations work on a similar principle, organizing and reorganizing as external influences bring new ideas and challenges, in tension with the fundamental nature or 'being' of who they are and what they stand for. So likewise, church is a fluid and ever-moving system, a very complex system, which is the result of the ongoing conversation between its essence and the environment in which it is set. Churches also 'carry their history on their backs' – every single, diverse and various, expression of them.

And this is so much of the problem with the word 'church'. We hear the word as if all the context and narrative contained within any expression of Christian community has been stripped out and boiled down into some generic image, often a pew-stuffed building with a dot-matrix congregation awaiting a venerable cleric. There is no context, no narrative, no complexity, no sense of what this phenomenon was *or might become*.

Church is not a 'thing'. It cannot be reduced down to some set of basic practices or principles and then built back up again like a machine. Bentley showed us that snow was not a thing that could be reduced to a single formula or diagram. He revealed it to be a wonder of complexity, a myriad marvel of diversity and emergent beauty whose full nature cannot be removed from its particular context.

We still use the word snow. But perhaps Bentley's work means that we use it with a more varied, humble and provisional imagination of what we mean when we say it. The same might be said of the word 'church'. We will continue to use it. But let the word 'church' be open to the possibility of its becoming, of it confounding our dull sense of what it has always been and surprising us with new ways of being what it might be, now and in the future.

As I turn the car toward home I pass again the cricket pavilion overlooking the neatly mown and rolled outfield of the ground. Just inside the boundary rope, a large tree stump, a recent victim of winter storms, punctuates the far side of the cricket pitch. Beyond it, through a scattering of mature oaks and beeches which together have that characteristic look of the country estate, lies one of the manor houses where the story of Great Melton parish began.

In the neat world of rural estates the lines were drawn clearly. Two churches, metres apart, existed for hundreds of years with a parish boundary between them. A line on an ecclesial map. A division in the imagination of those attending worship in either building that shaped the possibilities and limits of Christian community. But lines are blurring. Great Melton is less linear now, more complex.

It is the space beyond the boundary rope, among the long grass, where the possibility of reimagination lies. It is the edge places where the seeds of a new system can take root. Where the future is given flesh and form, free from the machine-like censorship of routine practices, the mowing of the lawns in neat lines, as beautiful and ordered as they may be. 'The new belongs elsewhere.' It must inhabit the wild edges for a time, the rented spaces, the unlikely places, while yet remaining alongside the boundary of the old, keeping open the conversation. Until boundaries cease to be boundaries.

Notes

1 Addison, *Movements That Change the World.*
2 Act 17.6 (NRSV).
3 Stark, *The Rise of Christianity.*
4 Kreider, *The Patient Ferment of the Early Church*, p. 9.
5 Kreider, pp. 8–9.
6 Koyama, *Three Mile an Hour God*, p. 7.
7 Swinton, *Becoming Friends of Time*, p. 81.
8 Koyama, *Three Mile an Hour God*, p. 6.
9 Swinton, *Becoming Friends of Time*, p. 74.

10 Archbishop's Council, *Mission-Shaped Church*, p. vii.
11 Taylor, *The Go-Between God*, p. 18.
12 Campbell, *Fifty Words for Snow*.
13 Bentley and Humphreys, *Snow Crystals*.

8

East Holme Priory, Dorset

This poem is a dissident church.
It broke out of prison.
It doesn't conform,
But whispers through the walls
To those who hear.
It won't take form
For the sake of dignity.
One day it might birth a movement
And ride bareback into the Kingdom of God.[1]

IN THE FULLNESS OF TIME

It is early summer and I am tasting warmth and light with a renewed gratitude following the restrictions of the long first lockdown of the global pandemic. The energy released by this liberation takes me to venture out to East Holme on the other side of Poole Harbour to reflect, pray and try to make some sense of the shape of my ministry in the new landscape that appears to be forming. East Holme Priory presents as a classic English manor house, set back from a wooded lane, overlooking traditionally fenced fields studded with grand mature oaks. I turn from the lane and head up the gravelled drive that bends from the road, flanked by high hedges of laurel and yew until the house is revealed, glowing in the sun. This is a house with a long and eclectic history. A house that still acts as a centre around which land and livestock, people and place orbit in the small constellation of houses and farmsteads of this Dorset village.

Hidden in plain sight, Dorset has a great many historic monastic centres which formed a significant part of the life of the church before the Reformation. One such place was East Holme Priory, a cell linked to the huge Cluniac monastery at Montacute just over the county border in Somerset. East Holme Priory has been in the ownership of the Bond family for generations. My own connection with it has developed through the welcome of Hilary, who married into the Bond family and lives there with her husband and family. Hilary is an ordained pioneer minister working within the parish. She is developing missional community among spiritual seekers and helping in the continued ministry of a community café on Wareham High St.[2]

There is little evidence of the monastic history of East Holme Priory now. Its name is the only obvious clue to its spiritual past. But there are traces and signs that start to open a deeper story of spirituality, prayer and witness in this place. A hoard of Roman coins discovered at East Holme is thought to have been a 'votive' hoard, suggesting that this was the site of a Roman temple. The Cluniac cell was established in the twelfth century and lasted until the dissolution in the sixteenth century.

Hilary tells me of a window in the kitchen whose stonework and tracery suggest it was reinstalled there from the ruins of the old monastery. The house itself was built on the site of the monastery and a priory church remained, acting as the parish church until the mid-eighteenth century when it became dilapidated and was removed. A new church was built in 1865, in the grounds of the house and accessed through the private drive. It remains a place of public worship and is part of the ministry of the parish of Wareham.

Extraordinarily the existence and site of the priory church was lost until very recently, when an archaeology student researched the grounds of the house and confirmed the existence of the old church and its location. And it's this site that the priory church occupied that now provides a shaded space in the lee of the house for barbecues and firepit conversations that form the basis of the small community Hilary is hosting. Beyond that space, the gravel drive leads the curious out towards the fields of the estate and round to the new parish church, adorned with the hand-painted Scripture verses and decorations of a former Lady Bond, its humble rows of pews still sanctuary for a small monthly gathering for Anglican worship.

In the warmth of the summer sun, I settle in to spend a day in this place of prayer. One of the large oaks in the parkland of the estate has come down in a recent storm. From where I sit, I watch as heavy machinery is brought in to dig out its roots and cart the ancient trunk away. We are still in the storm of the pandemic, churches remain closed and worship, with impressive creativity and speed, has set up online. And yet while we have proved to ourselves that a crisis such as a global pandemic can be navigated by our ingenuity and technology, there remains a deep sense of anxiety about the future. Income has plummeted without in-person worship. Revenue streams from the hire of halls have dried up. The existential threat to the church from its decline in resources suddenly feels more acute. Into that space examples of new Christian community at the edges of the institution find their stories gaining more traction than before. There is resonance with simple expressions of Christian community in the home and street, as home groups become churches meeting in back gardens and people rediscover their neighbours and work alongside them to care for those in need in their community. There is a growing sense that we are being invited to see something of what the church could be, what the church needs to be, to engage with those we live among. There is a growing sense that the sheer energy demanded of our gathered practice of church is preventing us from engaging meaningfully with our communities.

These were the themes of a complex and turbulent moment in time. I read my journals from the previous years, listening to those things I felt that God has spoken to me as I wrestled with a desire to follow his Spirit of mission in the ministry he has called me to. Strands and inklings of the voice of God echoed from those pages, and a coherency, perhaps inspired by that sense of a hinge in the continuum of time, began to coalesce into something. A poem? A prophecy? A vision? Something more like a piece of Old Testament prophetic writing. Not the prophecy of ecstatic utterance, but crafted prayerful literature in the midst of history and within the call of God to seek his presence and communicate his voice. The prophetic gift is the lingering presence of the Spirit on those with a call to stay attentive to the voice of God in relation to the world around them. Prophecy is the fruit of that attentiveness and its craft into language that can connect with insight and hope.

By the end of the day I had a piece of writing. I got up from the summer house, walked toward the house with its traces of ancient Christian movements long gone, past the site of the Priory church and through the set of gates toward the existing parish church of today. In that church, where worship is a regular but increasingly infrequent practice, within a large benefice team ministry stretched to lead services across a wide area, I placed what I had written on the altar. I stood there in that small insignificant place, conscious of its precariousness as a living place of worship and witness, and prayed that what was conveyed in what I had written might yet prove to have some insight and value for the future of the church.

EAST HOLME PRIORY, DORSET

This is what the Spirit says to the church in the UK:

Ancient forms are dying and falling apart
A tide is running and its current is strong.
A fire is burning and will not die out.
Cathedrals will fall, their walls crumbling and
  roofs collapsing.

But when you see the old forms die, do not be afraid.
Lament. Cry and mourn for the loss of these forms
For all that was beautiful, reliable and good.
For all that gave people safe passage through centuries of life.
Lament. But do not hold on.
Let go and stand empty-handed – for where else can we go?

A new church is being built nearby. A church without
  a footprint.
A church in which the cry of ordinary people is heard
Saying 'We are the church!'
A church that is local and ordinary; village, street,
  hearth, table.
A church birthed through the calling of the four winds
  of the Spirit
The Spirit from the north, south, east and west.
And these are the four winds:
Prayer – a community founded on a rhythm of prayer.
People of God – a community of the faithful followers of the
  Way, without more distinction.
Practices of the Kingdom – a community practising the
  disciplines of the teaching of Jesus.
Participation in the mission of God – a community
  discerning the initiative of God in the world
and joining in.

The world needs more than hospital ships
The world needs lifeboats, and lots of them,
Numerous, small, agile, local and available.

The world cries out for a way in the wilderness
For communities of hope in the midst of decline and despair.
The world needs a new Benedict.
It is looking for Francis.
Not primarily in the guise of a building or a brand
But in the loving gaze, the compassionate presence of
   a local community
Founded on the worship and way of Jesus.

I have the privilege of being witness to a few of what I am sure are 'communities of hope', 'local communities ... founded on the worship and way of Jesus'. By God's grace and the movement of the Spirit we are perhaps at the beginnings of a movement that will see many of these 'small, agile, local and available' communities spring up in all sorts of contexts alongside inherited forms of church.

John Good, a Baptist pioneer minister, came to Poole following an invitation to come and live in an area of new housing. Through praying, listening and building links with the local community his ministry took an unexpected turn. He found that for a lot of people in the local community getting out on the water of Poole Harbour was a key part of life: 'Water was really precious to people, it was really special.' And yet for some there were challenges in being able to access the water and make it part of their lives. And out of that conversation with the community, the idea of a library of watersports equipment emerged, basically a library of equipment that people could borrow at a reasonable price to enable them to access the water.[3] From these beginnings and connections John has been able to journey with people in exploring the connections between water and well-being and between water and spirituality. Most recently a missional community of 20–30 people has developed within this network of people, which currently goes under the name of Ocean Church. At first it has been a monthly gathering for worship on the water, but it aims to be not simply a kind of adapted 'church on the water' but a 'pattern of living' that enables the community to disciple one another in the midst of life together.

Likewise Ben Lucas, another Baptist Pioneer minister in Dorset, began with prayer and listening in the village of Charlton Down near Dorchester. Ben asked three questions through that process: 'What is the cry of this community? How does the story of the Bible connect with that cry? What would it look like for a community of people to embody a biblical response to that cry?' The cry Ben and others discerned was a cry of brokenness and division. A deep sense that division had taken root within the community and that their response to it needed to be 'a community of others that refuses to split and disagree'. In response to that cry a missional community has developed which is seeking to live lives that demonstrate the possibility of unity, a disparate community of people that look to express the distinctiveness of forgiveness and reconciliation in the midst of this village.

Within the ongoing life of Reconnect, one of the 'hubs' is led by Lucy Bolster on Turlin Moor, a social housing estate on the edge of Poole. At the heart of this are two households, next door to each other, sharing a common garden, who live a rhythm of prayer together. From this platform all sorts of things have been tried to offer a place of welcome and community to people in the locality. One expression of this that seems to connect is a shared meal on a weekday evening in which Bible stories are told and explored together. Prayer is expressed in simple, creative and participative ways. Through this rhythm of shared life, and a deep presence in the life of the wider community, people are finding a place in the shared story of faith and around a shared table.

And now at East Holme, above the invisible footprints of the original priory church, Hilary Bond has been drawing a community together around a firepit. The group shares stories and explores faith together. Hilary is not sure if this is a missional community or not. Many who come are Christians who are not currently attending a church of any kind. Some are people on a spiritual journey, open to exploration. What Hilary is concerned to do is create a space where people can bring any questions, no matter how daft, and where the experience and perspective of anyone who comes is valued.

None of those leading these communities are following a rubric, rolling out a model or applying a formula. What we may be witnessing is a move of God's Spirit that is inviting all sorts of people into a space in which there is greater freedom to express something of the heart of the New Testament church in the midst of the lives of their local communities. Implicit in this is a greater freedom from the anxiety of the institution to provide for its own survival. And there is a greater sense of commitment and patience for the long-term to see these missional communities enter into genuine mutual relationship with their communities in seeking fullness of life together.

※

John, Ben, Lucy, Hilary and myself found some time to explore this together. I asked them all what was distinctive for them about leading the kind of expression of church we are exploring. As we talked two words resolved from our conversation.

First – freedom. As ordained leaders within their respective institutions each of these folk has, through a mixture of determination and invitation, found the freedom to inhabit a different paradigm of mission and church. This was described as 'the freedom to be different' (Hilary) and therefore the freedom to be fluid and to adapt and change (Lucy), the freedom to experiment. But also a freedom from some of the accumulations and accretions of the tradition that enables a refounding of the church which is more rooted in relationships and the common experience of life together. There are no inventions here in the way that church is being expressed, no radical insights. Rather, the freedom to recover the heart of the apostolic vision of the church in the midst of the contemporary world. The principles that have informed the missional community in Charlton Down, for example, are 'the same as church' but the experience has been that 'they're much more beautiful and deeper when we're free' (Ben). Freedom too for people, including those leading these communities, to bring their whole selves into the life of the church community. By placing church as a community in the midst of place and integrated into the ordinariness of life, church cannot be performed or reduced to an event or action. Being church means that the gathering we call 'church' is the sum total of our lives as scattered Christian witnesses in the community. It is also the freedom to participate, 'to either be the person giving or receiving' and 'the freedom to be vulnerable' (Hilary). It is in essence the range of freedoms made possible by the refounding of Christian community on human relationship in the context of our relationship to God and to our community. A refounding that frees us from concepts of church that often encourage disconnection from time and place by their reduction of church to some sort of 'doing' rather than 'being'.

Second – mutuality. Within each community that develops from the leadership of these folk there is mutuality of leadership and participation. It might be described as a 'different power dynamic' which is based on participation and conversation within the community. The life and development of the community is held 'in-between', with 'power rolling between one another' (Lucy). It's a kind of 'osmosis ... a give and take, between everybody' such that 'everybody within a missional community can be the person who is giving or receiving' (Hilary). This kind of mutual and open conversation is a value within the missional community, a part of the DNA of its life. So it extends to the way in which such a community relates to its context. So often, as a church with a deep habit of being the church 'for' its community, we maintain a kind of client-provider relationship with those 'outside' the church. There is a conversation with our communities, but the topic and the language of the conversation are set by us. We are in control of the conversation.

Those leading missional communities seek to inhabit a different kind of posture with the community, one that enables an open conversation.

This posture of openness and mutuality became evident as we talked about mission. For some the language of mission is associated with the way in which the church has done mission 'to' its community. It has come with an agenda or a plan and has at times imposed that on a community. The kind of posture expressed here integrates mission much more with the 'being' of the church, the patient, local witness of a Christian community in the midst of its community. So a missional community might have a 'mission field that's just kind of wherever I am' (Hilary). Mission is life. 'Every day is a personal life being lived in such as way that it shines. And so in a way we're less aware of who our mission field is' (Ben).

This is a relationship that Lucy describes as 'being with one another with delight'. It means that the instinct of the missional community is to immerse its life without expectation amid the lives of those around it. It means an intentional but patient discipline of being a local expression of Christian community within the complex conversation of life in a context, trusting God to use that in his mission there. Ben describes the posture of their missional community as 'a desire to live in such a way that the Lord might trust us with the most broken and vulnerable in society'. Mission and church are the fruit of the life and witness of a community. We don't 'do' mission or even 'plant' a church. Mission and church are what happens when a group of people seek faithfully and openly to live lives of Christian discipleship in the full gaze of a community: 'the outcome of living well, the side effect of that is mission'. He quotes some advice given to him starting out: 'You don't plant churches, you just live your life, and then you realize one day that you've got a church.'

Mission is therefore an extension of a mutual and open conversation into the community. There is a deep attention to the presence of God in the community and to the ways in which people in the community are exploring life and making connections with God. John referred to Vincent Donovan's book *Christianity Rediscovered*, with its beautiful story of a developing expression of Christianity among the Maasai. Donovan's mission develops through an open conversation that initially sees him, as John puts it, 'learning the icons and language and the way of speaking in a culture'. Donovan connects with the people of the Maasai as fellow travellers and explorers of the person of God. Only through the patient process of listening and learning first is Donovan then able to bring his own experience into conversation with theirs.[4] So likewise, as John shares life with people out on the water in Poole Harbour he is starting a conversation. One that begins with a question: 'What does spirituality mean to somebody who goes outside to encounter whatever they feel it is that's "spiritual"?' What is forming from that conversation is a missional community that attempts to be shaped by that conversation, seeing the experiences and insights of those they are connecting with as a gift to the community in its growth and development.

Together Lucy, Hilary, Ben and John create a picture of new emergent communities that have found freedom and the space to experiment with a more mutual culture of life within the missional community, a culture that then flows out into its life in the wider community. And along with communities like Bardney, the Garden Churches springing up in villages in Norfolk and other networks of small communities, it does feel like we are witnessing a renaissance of small, intentional communities not unlike those that have sprung up at other times of significant cultural upheaval in the history of the church. It's too early to say where this is leading. But as Ben put it: 'History tends to show that revival happens on the edges. But the fruit of revival is the renewal of the inherited church.'

There's an urban myth that does the rounds from time to time about the development of the space pen. During the space race of the 1960s NASA realized that ordinary pens would not work in zero gravity. They consequently set about developing one and spent millions of public funds and a great deal of time developing a zero-gravity pen for its space missions. The Russians, faced with the same challenge – used pencils.[5]

It's a good story and a popular one, perhaps because it shines a light on the false sense of superiority we frequently get from our wealth and technical developments, often at the expense of common sense. It also a story that wants to remind us that while we are capable of the most sophisticated solutions to the most intractable problems, sometimes the answer to our problems lies in our hands. Or at least in our pencil case.

Around the same time as the moon landings a Church of England Bishop called John Taylor was reflecting on a similar issue in regard to the church. As computers and other technology began to become available to the church he saw the dangers of putting too much faith in them. Technology gives us great power and reach, but at what expense? 'We have instruments to enable us to see everything from the nebulae to the neutron,' he said 'Everything, except ourselves.'[6] The ability to reach beyond ourselves with the tools of technology may well prevent us from seeing, and using, what we already have if only we thought to notice.

So there are risks and dangers with technology and yet there are potentially huge rewards. The church has embraced all manner of technologies from the printing press to the radio, the television and now the internet as means of extending its reach. During Covid the technology of the internet and applications such as Zoom and Facebook Live have proved invaluable in enabling the church to function in such a challenging time. Lots of churches testified to huge numbers of people connecting with their online service broadcasts, often in greater numbers than their existing in-person congregations. Do we therefore simply need to engage more intentionally with technology, with the digital revolution, and with the generations that have grown up knowing nothing else except this digitally connected world? Or is there a danger that in doing so we have lost sight of the fundamental means by which we are invited to engage with the world – the people around us, those with whom we share our daily living, working, eating, recreational lives? And might we have put such trust in our podcasts, our Instagram feeds and our online services that we have lost sight of the God in our midst?

I say this to raise a question that seems to me to be one that's constantly raised by the Bible. Where do we put our trust? In our own technical ingenuity and that of the world around us, or in God? It's a theme that comes around again and again, in particular at times of great social upheaval. And one such time was in the transition from the time of the Judges to the establishment of the first kingdoms under Saul and David. In this chapter in the story of Israel, a story told in 1 and 2 Samuel, the narrative takes us from the people of God as a confederacy of different tribes to a nation under one king and one God.[7]

In this story the desire for a king is described as a dilemma. The people say they want a king in order to be like all the other nations around them.[8] Samuel, already old and with his power and influence waning, warns them what a king will do. He describes to them the dark side of monarchy in close detail. But it does no good. They still want a king. And so (reluctantly perhaps?) God tells Samuel to give them a king.

What might have happened if the people of God had not chosen a king? Was it inevitable that the political innovations of others – a authoritarian king holding power over a people and a territory – would be embraced by Israel? We'll never know, but it's clear from the way 1 Samuel is written that the writer didn't see a king as inevitable, or good. However, the author of 1 Samuel is too subtle to argue one way or another. What they want us to do is reflect long enough to ask what is truly important.

Likewise we are in a major cultural upheaval in our own time. The current state of flux may well be as significant as the Reformation or the end of the 'dark ages'. It may well be true that every 500 years or so we experience what Phyllis Tickle called a 'great semi-millennial rummage sale of ideas'.[9] Pope

Francis has said 'We are not living in an era of change, but a change of era.'[10] Of course, only time will tell to what extent the age we live in will be seen as era-defining. But it certainly feels that way. We live in an age virtually defined by change and by a sense that the norms by which the world, and the church, used to work are no longer dependable.

In such times of flux we look for something to start to hang the future on. Israel wanted a king. They wanted the political system that seemed to work for everyone else. It was surely a no-brainer for them to have one as well. Yet it is on this straightforward take on the dilemma that the writer of 1 Samuel weaves his subversive story. It's a story of the weak and the ordinary and the unqualified as the means by which God moves his story of salvation forward.

We start with Hannah, a barren woman, accused of drunkenness, whose prayers for a son are answered. That son, Samuel, dedicated to the temple as a toddler, hears the voice of God long before Eli the priest thinks it's possible. Once established as the prophet of Israel, Samuel is tasked with choosing someone from among the people to be king. His choice eventually rests on Saul who, as he says himself, is from the smallest tribe and the weakest clan. Saul is cast as an ambiguous character. He is from humble origins and without apparent ambition to rule yet he is nevertheless 'a head taller than any of the others'.[11]

And then we come to David and the pattern and the choice continues, between the anointing of a person of character irrespective of origins and the thirst for a person of power and stature. David is the youngest. He's not considered a possible candidate by his father Jesse. He's an afterthought, brought in from the fields where his life has been marked out for him as shepherd to the family flocks. And yet it is on David that the anointing rests.

Then David comes to the battlefield with the Philistines, where Jesse's older sons are stationed, and sees the situation with Goliath entirely differently. Faced with a warrior of such power and technical ability the Israelites have offered promises of reward for anyone willing to fight and kill him – wealth, status, tax-exemption! But David's not interested in any of that. And having persuaded Saul that despite his age he has the skills necessary to fight Goliath, David prepares to engage him in combat.

This part of the narrative is usually called the story of David and Goliath. But really it's the story of David *or* Goliath. Because, in placing this epic battle between a skinny youngster and the power and strength of Goliath, the writer of 1 Samuel is setting up the essential choice that Israel is making. Which way does Israel go? Do they go with the power and technical weaponry of Goliath? Do they try and fight toe to toe with the powers of the day on their terms? Or do they go with the unlikely, the weak, the counterintuitive and at times downright unreasonable approaches of the Lord God of Israel?

This dilemma is made clear in the choice of weaponry that David makes. Saul prepares David for the fight by getting him geared up in his own battledress but David, after showing a bit of willing, makes it clear that he can't fight Goliath in such weighty and ill-fitting gear. Instead, he goes with his instinct, his experience and what's around. He prepares to face Goliath in probably the same way he would have prepared to face a day looking after the family sheep. He takes his staff in his hand and heads for the stream where he chooses 'five smooth stones'. He places the stones in his shepherd bag and takes his sling shot and approaches Goliath.

The rejection of the standard weaponry of warfare at the time and the deliberate choice to go with what seems woefully underpowered for such a contest speaks volumes. The choices David makes are not a wholesale rejection of technology and power – as David's story develops we see his role as military leader grow. However, it seems to me that the writer of this history is posing a deep question about the blind ways in which we embrace the standard powers of technology in our day. The story invites us to consider that there might be other choices. For the people of God the reach for power and technology is not a given.

So this choice that David makes acts a metaphor for the kind of church we might choose to be in our call to be God's agents of mission in the world. In which case, what might this metaphor suggest to us? First, David's choice works within the grain of who he is. He is not a warrior, he is a shepherd boy. He's not going to pretend to be a warrior in borrowed armour and a heavy sword in his young hands. He chooses to work within the givenness of who he is and the experience he brings from his time in the fields. Are there times too for the church when we seem to adopt too readily what the world has to offer and forget who we really are? When we get so enticed by the shiny promises of technology that we lose sight of where we have come from, the value of the experience and tradition that we have to bring?

Second, having made the choice to go with his own experience, David makes another choice – five smooth stones. Presumably there were lots of stones in the stream bed that day. David chooses five. This might be purely pragmatic. Maybe he only has enough room in his shepherd's bag for five stones. Perhaps he thinks he can fire off five stones in quick succession before it's too late. Perhaps his experience suggests that out of five he will certainly strike once where he needs to. But he chooses five, which seems a large enough yet small enough number for my purposes in distilling some key choices, key practices for being small missional communities in our day.

David chose *smooth* stones. Some of the stones at the bed of the stream were too heavy, some too small, some too irregular to fly true in the air. As anyone who has skimmed stones on a calm lake or river will know, the choice of a good stone in these circumstances is a significant step towards a successful outcome. The fact that they were smooth probably has a pragmatic explanation. But stones are smooth because of the wearing of their surface over time. They are the result of long and patient processes which blunt awkward shapes and often bring out the beauty and colour of the original rock. For me they act in the story as symbols of experience, wisdom, tradition. All of which are undervalued and often maligned in our day where the novel is idolized and anything even a few years old has already ceased to have value. What then are the five smooth stones for missional community? What practices in the Christian story and experience, that have been worn and shaped by the ministry and experience of others down the centuries, might we want to choose for the challenge of mission in our own day?

This is something I've thought long and hard about through the ups and downs of my own experience of reaching out in mission to my own community. For myself and others this is not a wholesale critique of the congregation or the parish system or of a programmatic approach to mission and ministry. It is, however, a call of God, by his Spirit, to embrace a mode of mission and being church that holds a promise for the future and draws on the experience and practice of the past. I believe that the writer of 1 Samuel wants to draw Israel back to its foundations – to weakness, vulnerability and a dependence on God. At the same time there is a pragmatism that recognizes the developments in their communal life – kings, territory, professional armies, political alliances. These things must be held together.

The five smooth stones are the distillation of the wisdom, experience and practice of missional community. I want to lay out a case for these practices as equivalents to David's five smooth stones. They are carefully chosen, long in the making, with a grain and patina that look back to the recurring intentional communal forms of the church's past. When used effectively and with conviction I believe they have the power to challenge the forces facing the church in its mission today.

1 **Small** – Christian community that is small enough to enable us to be 'one another',[12] to adapt quickly to the changing world around it, to be participative and foster belonging.
2 **Slow** – Christian community that rejects the accelerating pace of modern life with its events and programmes that must always be better and more popular than the last, that doesn't exhaust people, that moves on average at a human pace, the pace of love, and the pace that allows for the voice of God to be heard.
3 **Simple** – Christian community that is earthed in people's lives, the kitchen table, the back garden, the cafe and the

street, that holds lightly to the heavy burdens of buildings and staff teams and is therefore simple enough for relationships to remain the priority.
4 **Sent** – Christian community that is consciously in the world in the name of the One who sends – local and deeply attentive to its context, not imposing its own agenda, not meeting a perceived need on its own terms, but joining in with the story of a place to help make authentic connections between the life of a community and the good news of the Gospel.
5 **Serving** – Christian community that serves the missionary Spirit of God and therefore serves its local community and serves the desire that people have for fullness of life and for loving relationships with one another, the creation and with God through Jesus Christ.

These principles have their roots in two important interconnecting themes of theology. First, the incarnation, which argues for an expression of Christian life of such a form that it can remain engaged in the ordinary life of the world. One that is not so complex or structured that the power of its own gravity draws it away from the world. But instead one that is open and vulnerable enough to remain needful of relationships with the world. 'The world' said John V. Taylor, 'is the church's milieu.'[13] In other words, the church needs the world. It cannot afford itself the luxury of being so self-sufficient, or indeed so dominant, that either it retreats from the world or completely 'churches' the world. Jesus' call of humble, ordinary, uneducated folk from the forgotten corners of Judea seems a pretty deliberate strategy to found the church in a posture of humility and vulnerability towards the world.

Second, the principle of the *missio Dei*. The understanding that mission is a characteristic of the nature of God, not something that God chooses to do in addition to who he is. Mission is not a 'second step' for God but an intrinsic part of the nature of God's being. It flows from this that the church is not *the* missionary agent of God in the world, without which God's mission would be nullified. God's presence in the world ensures his ongoing mission, which he graciously invites the church to participate in.

The Acts of the Apostles is a poorly named book. While it narrates much of what the early church did, the testimony of its narrative is of a church desperately trying to keep up with the activity of the Spirit of God. Acts tells the story of the church being formed by the Spirit as the Spirit forms the church and then draws it into the unfolding drama of its own development, from Jerusalem to the end of the earth. To be the church, before anything that the church might do, is to be drawn into that life of God that is for the world. For the world in its particularity, its place and people, its multiplicity and mundanity, its beauty and brokenness.

Yet while these two theological strands have informed the practice of missional community, the five principles that they identify have also been distilled from ongoing practice. Out of the messy reality of things that have been tried and failed and others that have developed and been sustained, these principles have won through. They have emerged as the result of the conversation between experience, these theological convictions and a constant cross-referencing with the church's story through history. They are an attempt to make sense of our experience that has emerged from our own practice and that helps articulate what is distinctive about these small forms of Christian community within the wider ecology of the church. These principles may not be articulated in quite the same way in every context, but as I travel and visit other movements and expressions of missional community in other places, some of which are represented in this book, I see them expressed again and again. Perhaps, then, they are principles whose time has come. Five smooth stones for missional community in a secular age.

It's a cold, blandly overcast day and I stop on the road out toward the wilds of Cranborne Chase in east Dorset and wander around the site of Knowlton Church. For years I saw and ignored this hollowed-out ruin set back from the road. Now I can hardly stop myself from paying another visit. It's late February and the verges and woodland clearings are streaked with flashes of snowdrops. The world is tilting into life again. The whirl and pull of stars and planets drawing life from the ground. Yet the ground feels dead. Cold, damp, lifeless. It remains a gift of faith to see the landscape green and productive once again.

I step inside the ring of fencing that marks this place as different, as a protected space from cattle, the tractor and the plough. Within this protective orbit lie the rings of Knowlton. Two banks of mounded earth with entrances east and west circling a wide central space, in the middle of which stands the ruins of a church. The rings are thought to have been constructed around 2500 BC and were probably for ceremonial use. Walking through the banks I am pulled to the centre and to the church. A Norman church stood here, was remodelled in the fourteenth century, before falling into disuse in the seventeenth century. It has all the familiar proportions and shape of any number of similar churches nearby. But time has not been kind. The tower and nave stand open to the sky. The east window has been cleaved and chewed, its shape and form lost to the attrition of the elements.

Entering the church through the arch of the old south door there is a tower to my left and the familiar shape of a sanctuary to my right. At the bottom of the tower someone has left a single rose and two red votive candles. There has been no official worship here for perhaps 400 years. Yet 'buildings have a ministry'. Perhaps a significant one, unseen, unheralded. Thin places in the landscape of time in which the significance of our lives and that of others can be placed.

From the tower base I turn, look down the open nave to the vacant altar space and beyond the shattered window to the Neolithic entrance eastwards. There, two yew trees, those ancient, sacred trees, stand sentry. They draw me, as they always do. For they are no longer passed by as markers at the edge of things. No longer are they a gateway to the focus of the church. They are now an altar in themselves. Within the calm, deep green space at their base these trees now host a sacred space. Coloured streamers hang from the branches, candles and messages have been placed at their base. There are small soft toys, stones with prayers scrawled on them, flowers and other artefacts tucked into smooth hollows of the yew bark. I have been coming to Knowlton on and off for over five years and this place of worship has been renewed each time. It is a living focus for the desires of people to seek the spiritual in an age quietly rejecting the assumptions of the modern materialist world. The future is meeting the past, and the past the future, in the shade of these centuries-old trees.

It's hard to look back at the church from this viewpoint and not see it as peripheral, irrelevant even, its walls disappearing slowly into the soil, its place at the centre dislodged. The edge might be the centre now. Though what it is the centre *of* no-one is really quite sure. But while history, social change and human endeavour placed Christianity as the world view of the land, making a solid centre of a porous circle, the centre hasn't held. Spiritually we are a galaxy of possibilities, a 'nova effect'[14] of searchings and questings into the wilds of the spiritual universe. Our buildings still inhabit the land, there are still flowers placed in the stillness of their sacred spaces, but on nearby trees the spirituality of secular Britain flutters in the breeze.

I come to Knowlton now as a kind of spiritual discipline. I come to pray for the church in the county of my birth, the county in which I have now spent the majority of my life. I come to pray in the context of the spiritual reality of our age. And I come to pray in the context of time, deep time. Prayers shaped in a place full of the relics of a pre-Christian past and the reality of a post-Christendom future. And I come to Knowlton to pray and put my own human endeavours in the perspective of the fullness of time. Allowing the long turbulent view of history to refine my hopes and dreams for the church.

There are two reflections that walking and praying through the history of Knowlton bring to my ministry and to my thoughts on the place of the church. First, that church exists in liminality. Time is the milieu of the church. The experience of the people of God is an experience of pilgrimage, of always being between one time and one place and another, always leaving and always arriving. Always leaving the past and finding in the future the way to live hopefully in the present. The church is always walking, 'walking backwards into the future'[15] perhaps. Deeply mindful and honouring of the wisdom and tradition of the past. And yet walking in the power of the Spirit that comes, as it were, from the future, from the end of the journey, inviting us to step confidently and imaginatively in that direction. So the invitation to the church is to be a people of the tent not the temple. Places like Knowlton are painful but important reminders that temples are a risk. A misadventure in time. Temples are an attempt to ignore the arrow of time, to staunch the dynamic flow of history. And they place at risk that call to follow the Spirit into a world that has tilted once more around its temporary axis and where the gravity at work on people's lives is drawing them away from, not toward, what was once perceived to be the centre.

Second, and as a consequence of the first, the church must always be regarded provisionally in the forms which it takes. We cannot take for granted that the form of the church that has nurtured us has some kind of sacred right to do the same for all people and all time. The church has expressed its core truth and purpose in all manner of forms in time and place, in various cultures and contexts since the day of Pentecost, each form emerging from that creative conversation that takes place between Scripture, tradition and the uniqueness of a cultural context. That is the nature of the church. These things we call churches 'emerge from the interaction of their cultural assumptions, the special historical inheritances and their understanding of God's revelation through Scripture'.[16] Places like Knowlton help us attend to the implicit variety of the church as it responds to the flow of time in a given place. 'Go back 600 years,' argues Rowan Williams, 'you'd have monasteries of different kinds. You'd have enclosed orders. You'd have friars, the preaching orders. You'd have local guild churches and parish churches and chantry chapels and cathedrals and minsters, not just the parish church. And we've airbrushed that variety out of the picture.'[17] Places like Knowlton warn us against crystallizing the church into any one form or expression. They keep us humble and yet hopeful. For where God by his Spirit has brought new expression to the form of the church God will do so again.

Knowlton, and places like it, also help me pray in the patient spirit of the early church. I am reminded, in this frantic, accelerating world, that the arc of God's grace is long and bends toward the Kingdom. Slowly. And not only slowly, but mysteriously. There are few straight lines in the geometry of the church's history. This is the nature of story. A story we inhabit as patient witnesses to the person of Jesus, who died and rose again, in place and in time. A story we inhabit passionately but patiently, confident that God will fulfil his purposes 'in the fullness of time'.

Notes

1 The first Baptist church in Dorset was started in Dorchester in 1645. Its first minister, Francis Bamfield, was arrested in 1662 and placed in Dorchester prison for breaking the rule which forbade ministers from preaching within five miles of their church. Bamfield formed a church community within the prison and each morning would preach to his congregation in the yard beside the walls of the church. Unknown to him his sermons could be heard beyond the walls of the prison. A crowd developed outside the prison wall each morning in order to hear Bamfield preach; https://dorchesterbc.org.uk/a-brief-history (accessed 8.2.24).

2 https://www.facebook.com/NotJustSundaes (accessed 8.2.24).

3 https://www.watersportslibrary.com/ (accessed 8.2.24).

4 Donovan, *Christianity Rediscovered*.

5 Sadly, this story doesn't quite line up with the facts. It's true that both the American and Russian space programmes recognized this as a challenge. It's also true that the early Russian cosmonauts commonly used pencils. However, a US company run by Paul Fischer independently developed a 'space-pen' that would work in zero gravity and patented the invention in 1965. The US started using these pens for their mission from 1967 onwards and by the late 60s both they and Russians had bought consignments of the Fischer pens for their space programmes.

6 Taylor, *The Go-Between God*, p. 69.

7 For an excellent series of reflections on leadership from the books of 1 and 2 Samuel see Runcorn, *Fear and Trust*.

8 1 Samuel 8.5.

9 Tickle, *The Great Emergence*.

10 In a 2015 address in Florence; see https://cruxnow.com/church/2015/11/pope-francis-says-catholics-must-be-open-to-change (accessed 8.2.24).

11 1 Samuel 9.2.

12 John V. Taylor argues for the significance of the term 'one another', used frequently in the New Testament when describing the early church. Taylor asked what kind of structure fosters the sort of participative life in the Spirit that these pictures evoke and guards against the tendency toward institutionalism and control. Taylor argues that the answer lies in the testimony of the early church, which displays a consistent participative quality throughout the New Testament. This can be seen in the word *allelon*, 'one another', which punctuates the New Testament 'like a peal of bells' (John V. Taylor, *The Go-Between God*, p. 126). Taylor goes on to argue that 'the ideal shape of the church is such as will provide this 'one-anotherness' with the least possible withdrawal of Christians from their corporateness with their fellow men in the world' (p. 148). That size and shape will therefore probably be small. Small enough to allow for 'one-another-ing' within and protecting against the alienating effect that large structuring inevitably brings. Taylor therefore argues for the renewal of the 'little congregations' as a shape and size of church that is better able to embody the participative spirit of the early church's witness of *allelon*.

13 From a CMS Newsletter, No. 267, January 1964, quoted in J. Baker and C. Ross, *Imagining Mission with John V. Taylor*, London: SCM, 2020, p.3.

14 Charles Taylor's *A Secular Age* refers to an explosion in possibilities and options for people exploring spirituality in the present day. Taylor says: 'We are now living in a spiritual super-nova, a kind of galloping pluralism on the spiritual plane' (p. 300). For a shorter, more accessible and highly readable take on Taylor's work see Smith (2014), *How (Not) to Be Secular*.

15 A phrase used by Archbishop Justin Welby in a joint Presidential address to the General Synod of the Church of England in July 2021. https://www.archbishopofcanterbury.org/speaking-writing/speeches/general-synod-joint-presidential-address-archbishops (accessed 8.2.24).

16 Duerksen and Dyrness, *Seeking Church: Emerging witnesses to the Kingdom*, p. ix.

17 Rowan Williams, quoted in Taylor, *First Expressions: Innovation and the mission of God*.

Further Resources

Poole Missional Communities offer a number of resources that seek to enable the church to reimagine its presence and witness in a local context.

Ember is for churches that are facing closure or having to rethink what church is. It's a space to be courageous and real about the decline of a church. Ember takes a church leadership team on a journey comprised of worship, reflection, honest conversation, prayer, story and support. It seeks to enable a church community to journey with God through the themes of Easter – Surrender, Death and Resurrection. The journey offers space and time to discern the heart of what God is calling a local church towards and to creatively reimagine what the future might be for them.

Table helps groups of Christians who sense a call to mission in their context to explore how they might share life and ministry together as a missional community. The resource is designed to be used with a team, either one that could form, is forming or has formed, as they meet together. The resource consists of five beautifully designed interactive sheets including quotes, questions, diagrams, images and information, which form the basis for a learning conversation together. Table will help a team form and grow through journeying together and through sharing thoughts and opinions honestly. It helps a team make decisions as they set out on the road together as a missional community.

For more information on these and other resources please visit: www.poolemc.org.uk/resources

Bibliography

Addison, Steve, *Movements That Change the World*, Downers Grove: IVP, 2009.
Aisthorpe, Steve, *The Invisible Church*, Edinburgh: St Andrews Press, 2016.
Arbuckle, Gerald, *Refounding the Church*, London: Geoffrey Chapman, 1993.
Archbishop's Council, The, *Mission-Shaped Church*, London: Church House Publishing, 2004.
Bentley, W. A., and W. J. Humphreys, *Snow Crystals*, New York: Dover, 1962.
Bevans, Stephen, 'The Church as the creation of the Spirit', *Missiology* 35 (1), 2007, 5–21.
Campbell, Nancy, *Fifty Words for Snow*, London: Elliot & Thompson, 2020.
Chan, Francis, *Letters to the Church*, Brighton: David Cook, 2018.
Chesterton, G. K., *Saint Francis of Assisi*, New York: Doubleday, 1924.
Colville, Robert, *The Great Acceleration: How the world is getting faster and faster*, London: Bloomsbury, 2016.
Donovan, Vincent, *Christianity Rediscovered*, London: SCM, 2001.
Duerksen, Darren T. and William A. Dyrness, *Seeking Church: Emerging witnesses to the Kingdom*, Downers Grove: IVP, 2019.
Eliot, T. S., *Four Quartets*, London: Faber and Faber, 1944.
Fanthorpe, U. A., *Selected Poems*, London: Pen, 1986.
Foulger, Will, *Present in Every Place?* London: SCM, 2023.
Francis, Lesley, 'Taking discipleship learning seriously; setting priorities for the rural church', *Rural Theology* 13(1), 2015: 18–30.
Jordan, Marie, *A History of Stour Row*, 2000.
Koyama, Kosuke, *Three Mile an Hour God*, London: SCM, 1979.
Kreider, Alan, *The Patient Ferment of the Early Church*, Grand Rapids, Michigan: Baker Books, 2016.
Newbigin, Lesslie, *The Gospel in a Pluralist Society*, Grand Rapids, Michigan: Eerdmans, 1989.
Paas, Stefan, *Church Planting in the Secular West*, Grand Rapids, Michigan: Eerdmans, 2016.

———, *Pilgrims and Priests: Christian mission in a post-Christian society*, London: SCM, 2019.
Priest, Barbara, 'Gone ... and Almost Forgotten', 2019.
Prigogine, Ilya, and Isabelle Stengers, *Order Out of Chaos*, London: Verso, 2017.
Root, Andrew, *The Congregation in a Secular Age*, Grand Rapids, Michigan: Baker Books, 2021.
———, *Churches and the Crisis of Decline*, Grand Rapids, Michigan: Baker Books, 2022.
Rumsey, Andrew, *Parish: An Anglican theology of place*, London: SCM, 2017.
Runcorn, David, *Fear and Trust*, London: SPCK, 2011.
Simard, Suzanne, *Finding the Mother Tree*, Dublin: Penguin, 2022.
Smith, James K., *How (Not) to Be Secular*, Grand Rapids, Michigan: Eerdmans, 2014.
———, *How To Inhabit Time*, Grand Rapids, Michigan: Brazos Press, 2022.
Stark, Rodney, *The Rise of Christianity*, New York: HarperCollins, 1996.
Swinton, John, *Becoming Friends of Time*, London: SCM, 2016.
Taylor, Charles, *A Secular Age*, Cambridge, Massachussets: Harvard University Press, 2007.
Taylor, John V., *The Go-Between God*, London: SCM, 1972.
Taylor, Steve, *First Expressions: Innovation and the mission of God*, London: SCM, 2019.
Tickle, Phyllis, *The Great Emergence*, Ada, Michigan: Baker Books, 2012.
Tree, Isabella, *Wilding*, London: Picador, 2018.
Wells, Sam, *A Future That's Bigger than the Past*, Norwich: Canterbury Press, 2019.
Wheatley, Margaret, and Deborah Frieze, *Walk Out Walk On*, San Francisco: Berkana, 2011.
Winter, Ralph, 'The two redemptive structures of God's mission', *Missiology* 2(1), 1974: 121–39.